ADVENTURE!

ADVENTURE!

BY CARVETH WELLS

WITH A FOREWORD BY

LOWELL THOMAS

illustrated

THE JOHN DAY COMPANY

NEW YORK

A PATHFINDER BOOK REPRINT EDITION
Complete and Unabridged

Printed in the United States of America

ISBN: 979-8-8691-4388-4

To My Son
J A C K
HITCH-HIKING HIS WAY
AROUND THE WORLD

FOREWORD

For a brief moment I want to present a picture of
an indignant Carveth Wells. Yes I know, Carveth is
not the indignant type. Anything so serious as indig-
nation whether righteous or otherwise, is foreign to
his genial temper. But this time he was a trifle miffed,
although he still couldn't help smiling. In fact, he
was laughing. He told me how in an address before
a mid-western audience he had told about the tree
climbing fish of the Malayan Jungle. That tree
climbing fish didn't seem to carry any great convic-
tion with the audience on Main Street, because when
Carveth had finished a man came up, mentioned the
Arboreal Piscatorian and said: "Well, you must
have also seen the Swaraj Fish out there?"

"What's the Swaraj Fish?" asked Carveth.

"Oh," responded the cynic, "haven't you heard
about that remarkable creature? Well, the Swaraj
Fish wears a loin cloth like Ghandi and makes salt.
Maybe you were the man who told the Tall Story
Club about it."

Well, I couldn't blame Carveth for being a trifle

annoyed, especially after an incident that had happened shortly before.

Carveth had given that same lecture on the outlandish strangeness of the Malay Jungle and after he was through, Professor Henry E. Crampton of Columbia University, who was in the audience, felt impelled to take the floor and declare: "I myself have seen this fish Carveth Wells tells about. I've seen them climb trees in the Malay Jungle. I have listened carefully to this lecture, and every word was scientifically and biologically accurate."

Adventure! is a remarkable book in a number of ways. But the thing I particularly like about it is that there is a thrill on one page and a laugh on the next.

The central fact is that Carveth Wells is a lighthearted explorer. He has done serious work in casting light upon the remote places of the earth, but he doesn't take any of it too seriously. He's gone through perils and hardships in some of the wildest outlands on this globe, but he takes that lightly too. The most nerve-wracking ordeal, the most bloodcurdling peril would be turned into a laugh by this gay blade of exploration. And that's where Carveth Wells is unique. I know platoons and regiments of explorers—they are all inclined to be a bit solemn about their exploits, and so it's a relief and delight

FOREWORD

to come across a man of adventurous travels who
keeps his eyes fixed on the funny side of it all, and
who even does a bit of wholesome debunking of
the grandiose profession of exploration.

LOWELL THOMAS

New York

PREFACE

It has always been my ambition to discover something that someone else hasn't discovered before! The trouble is that when I make such a discovery I am classed as a second Baron Munchausen. When I first came back from the Malay Jungle and told stories of fish that climb trees, of bouncing fish balls, of lizards that break off their tails, of singing earthworms, and bushes that lie down when they notice you coming, my audiences laughed and exclaimed, "What a delightful liar!" or "What a liar!"

It was not until I wrote my book *Six Years in the Malay Jungle,* the preface of which was written by Doctor Frederick Lucas, Director of the American Museum of Natural History, who vouched for the truth of all my "lies," that it occurred to people that, after all, I only had the faculty of making the truth *sound* like a lie.

It's an extraordinary fact that the world is full of people who become quite annoyed when they hear something they have never heard before. At a banquet given in honor of Nansen, General Greely, dean of arctic explorers, in introducing me to Nansen exclaimed, "You ought to hear Carveth Wells's

PREFACE

jungle stories. I'm sure you would never know whether to believe them or not. But you wouldn't care. They are fascinating."

Having "done" the Malay Jungle, I next visited the Arctic and instead of finding it a region of ice and snow, inhabited by Eskimos, polar bears, and walruses, I nearly died of the heat, was devoured by mosquitoes, and could find none of the inhabitants who had ever heard of an Eskimo. I had gone to Lapland in the summertime. I never could understand why the really great explorers have always insisted on visiting the Arctic in the winter. My account of the migration of lemmings, those tiny animals like guinea pigs which suddenly arrive in millions from heaven (see Encyclopaedia Britannica), and swim away into the ocean, seeking the Lost Continent of Atlantis, is still always received with roars of laughter and benevolent unbelief.

One day at the end of a strenuous lecture tour I sought refreshment in those Isles of Enchantment, the Bermudas, where I found that the principal flowers, birds, fish, and even the scenery were red, white and blue. These facts were so obvious that they had passed unnoticed even by the inhabitants of the islands.

And now Africa, darkest Africa, that frightful continent of man-eating lions, and snakes that spit poison ten feet, of bloodthirsty natives and terrible tsetse flies, seemed to be crying to me, personally, to debunk it. I started to read all the books on Central Africa I could find, from Stanley's *Darkest Africa,* to Streeter's *Denatured Africa.* The accounts were so conflicting that I decided to see the place for myself, and especially the terrible African "jungles" where so many marvelous motion pictures have been taken "at great danger to life" ever since Paul Rainey first showed his wonderful photographs of African wild life.

What did I find? As usual, the unexpected. The word "jungle" was actually never used but in its place "the blue," simply because central equatorial Africa is such open country that the horizon in any direction fades away in a haze of blue. The worst "jungle" that I saw in the lion country looked like an apple orchard!

I was actually snowbound on the Equator and found myself shivering with tropical fever in a hailstorm. My native carriers huddled round big fires to keep warm and at mealtime picked blackberries. It was a paradise for Scotsmen. Heather was fifty feet high! And what a place of plenty it would be for canaries, if only they knew that their favorite food, "groundsel," grew in gigantic forests thirty feet high. (See "groundsel," Encyclopaedia Britannica.)

PREFACE

If African parsley were used for garnishing beef-steak, dishes would have to be fifteen feet in diameter with a nice roast ox in the middle. Parsley was nine feet high!

We had no need for weather bureaus, as we controlled the weather with a flute played by a witch doctor. Lions were being chased around by Boy Scouts and the most dangerous animal in the country was the jigger, a small flea imported from South America! We fished for lions from motor cars and positively saw millions of fly swatters attached to the tails of gnus. When Aristotle said there were snowcapped mountains on the Equator he certainly knew his oats, because I not only found the mountains but on the top of one, the calling card of the Duke of Abruzzi, left there by him twenty-two years before! From the top of the Mountains of the Moon, I soliloquized on the "hardships" of Safari and overlooked the Great Unwashed. Africa was turned upside down. I had shaken the truth out of it!

This book contains no plot! Its "style" is my style. I claim no place for it on the bookshelves of the highbrowed!

It is merely a collection of incidents taken from my numerous notebooks, arranged, as far as possible, in chronological order.

Possessing no plot, you may open it where you will

PREFACE

and I hope that you will find something of interest and perhaps entertainment.

Should the reader find himself deriving a certain amount of information, I hope it will have been acquired painlessly!

If this book has any moral, it is this:

Don't stay in your own particular little groove! Get out if you don't like it.

Because you were trained to be a doctor, for instance, do not stick to doctoring if you can be happier selling apples! Because probably apple selling was what you were originally intended for.

Take a chance! You *must* be a gambler in life, if you wish to retain your individuality.

Fight, strive, keep smiling—in fact remember the old biblical injunction, "ask and ye shall have— seek and ye shall find—knock and it shall be open unto you."

Personally my mottoes are, *Carpe diem!*—"Seize the Day!", and "The Lord will provide!"

I wish to acknowledge my indebtedness to the publishers of *Asia Magazine* and the *Philadelphia Forum Magazine,* for permission to use material that has appeared in their columns. I acknowledge also my indebtedness to Mr Andrew A. Freeman for his invaluable editorial assistance.

CARVETH WELLS.

xvii

CONTENTS

CONTENTS

ILLUSTRATIONS

Topsy-Turvy Land

CHAPTER ONE

MY adventures began when as a youngster I bought apples from a Devonshire grocer.

On the strength of this I got up nerve to apply to Lord Halsbury, England's Lord Chancellor, asking him to recommend me for an engineering job in the colonies. He did not see why he should—until I told him that the grocer from whom I used to buy my apples was his brother. I got the job.

Some weeks later I landed in Malaya, a queer part of the earth that Darwin dubbed "Topsy-Turvy Land." I soon found out why, for in this strange country there is no change of season! Winter and summer are indistinguishable, the sun rising and setting on what seems unvaried schedule and though it may rain nine inches in the course of a morning, there is no wet or dry season.

The people, too, do things in topsy-turvy fashion. This Mongoloid race has complexions varying from nearly white to the shade of a strong cup of coffee. Of all these hues, yellow is considered the most beautiful. Both men and women wear skirts called sarongs which have neither buttons nor hooks nor strings. Parents never punish their children and youngsters do just what they please about eating, sleeping and going to school. When a boy wants a meal he can take a long stick, put a sort of glue on one end and catch dragon flies. Then he pulls off the wings, takes his catch home, and after frying the flies in oil, smothers them with shrimp and onions. If he gets sick it certainly is no one's fault but his own.

It may be that the "heat equator" which divides the country right in half, accounts for the upside-down condition of Malay life. I don't know. But I do know that nowhere else did I ever see a fish come out of a hole in the ground, skip blithely toward a tree, climb it and then—wink at me. Nor did I ever in any other part of the globe see any other fish suffer from the heat to such an extent that he would air himself in a tree and then, after climbing down, go to the edge of a pool and douse his head with water.

Nowhere else did I ever see a man send a monkey up a tree, tell him to throw down green or yellow coconuts, and get what he ordered. And no other land ever produced a boy with a gun marked "The

Tower of London, 1800," who threw bait into the water and then shot the rising fish with bullets as large as marbles.

This queer country is a mountainous peninsula through which streams and rivers galore make their way in every direction. The mountains are not higher than 8,000 feet, and in the luxuriant valleys is found the nearly pure tin which gives the world about half its present supply.

I arrived in Malaya not to mine tin but to survey a railroad, and of everything that ever happened to me in that equatorial peninsula nothing struck me harder than my first day on the job. Our working crew started downstream in two boats, and immediately we upset Malay tradition by racing. Any one who paddles downstream is considered out of his mind but we went down the river at a wild pace. Just as my boat was drawing close to the leader, the coolies in the first boat stopped paddling and began frantically to slap at the water. I did not understand the cause of their excitement until I saw a three-foot water snake change its course from their boat to ours. Despite our own frenzied slapping the snake got aboard, looked around and went right on into the water again over the other side. Later I learned that Malayan water snakes never swim a river without taking a good look at anything and everything they come across.

The jumping off place for our survey was a river bank clearing on the top of a fifty degree slope. Looking as hard as I could, I could see no farther than forty feet each way. The heat was terrific. Although one of my men held a big Chinese umbrella over my head as I looked through my level, the instrument got so hot that the spirit bubble shriveled to a tenth its ordinary size. The perspiration poured off me so furiously that every entry I made in my notebook was thoroughly drenched. Leeches slipped through the eyelets in my boots, got down into my socks and feasted on my blood. My skin burned to a brilliant red. And it took me five hours to cover a quarter mile. I learned much about the real Malay jungle from that survey. The decay of vegetable matter down through centuries and centuries has made of the dense forests an unbelievable tangle of vegetation. Trees and plants alike fight for light. Trees shoot straight up like telegraph poles and often reach 100 feet before spreading out into a large cabbage-like top. Orchids cover some of these trees from top to bottom, and rope-like vines, as long as 600 feet, stretch through the jungle. At the feet of the trees is the débris of the ages to a depth

—as I know from an attempt to sink a well—of more than a hundred feet.

Paths through the jungle are not many, and most of the main passes are elephant tracks. I surveyed several hundred miles of these, very often finding side and branch tracks. When a tree falls across a path, the natives cut a new track around the tree for the elephants and build a staircase over the log for themselves. Then every passer-by enlarges a notch in the fallen tree until finally the track is opened wide across the old path.

My servant once told me of seeing two elephants come to such a break in the path. The mother elephant went around the log, but her baby, in too much of a hurry to detour, dashed through the notched log and got stuck. He began to squeal for help, and mother provided it. Backing from the baby's stern, she swung into action and headed directly for the mark. Head down, she rammed the youngster with a solid thud and shot him on through the hole. Then she patiently walked around the log again.

The animals of this jungle are fascinating. Certainly no other forest could provide a deer which you attract by rattling two sticks upon a large leaf and which when shot, will go into your pocket. Yet the Malayan mouse deer, with a body the size of a small rabbit and with pencil-like legs, can be fried in an ordinary pan and served up as a single dinner portion. This little *plandok,* my servant used to tell me, escapes from tigers and leopards by jumping into the air and seizing a tree branch with the two sharp tusks in his upper jaw. He hangs there like fruit until his puzzled enemy goes away wondering how the little fellow vanished so completely.

Tigers, however, provide most of the excitement. The natives live in fear of these marauders and never mention the animal by name in the jungle. Women particularly are terrified by the tiger and speak most respectfully of him as "the old gentleman" or "his lordship." But the tiger himself is no respecter of either men or women.

One girl, who had come to the peninsula to be a hospital nurse, dragged her bed to the window of her room and opened the shutters to get the benefit of the cool night air. When she waked later she saw the huge head of a tiger peering in at the window. With unusual presence of mind, she flung her pillow at the animal which caught it in his paws and ripped it wide open. Upon eating it he almost choked, and was still trying to free himself of the feathers when a watchman shot him.

Night brings many tiger stories such as one told me by a young engineer. He had decided to sleep in the open because his tent was hot. He carried his cot some distance from camp and suspended the mosquito netting from a tree limb. He slept soundly until he felt something blowing hotter on his face than any wind. Two shining eyes met his. Then another pair of eyes joined the first pair at the mosquito netting. Around and around the netting the two tigers went. At length, with a wild yell, the engineer leaped from bed and fled for camp. The strange mosquito net had kept the tigers at bay, and the sudden shriek had frightened them back to the jungle.

Not all sleepers have been so fortunate as were the nurse and the young engineer. One of my own coolies was lying on a raised bench in a house along with twelve others. Next morning he had disappeared. A tiger had selected him as the best of the lot, and carried him off. We found his head, arms and legs a quarter mile from camp.

Though crocodiles prefer the rivers to the jungles, they seem to have the same desire for human food as tigers. I have seen an old man run madly through town with an enormous crocodile snapping a huge mouth at his heels. As they passed a police station, the crocodile met his end from a policeman's gun.

Crocodiles are clever. Usually they spot a prospective victim on the river bank, slip up behind him, and sideswipe him into the water with a flip of a powerful tail. Then, instead of making a meal at once, they poke the victim into the mud of the river bottom and let him drown while they rise to the surface and pretend to know nothing about what is going on. After a couple of weeks, the crocodile returns, pulls the body into pieces of munchable size, and stuffs his stomach comfortably full. Then he crawls on to a mud bank, stretches lazily out in the sun, and opens his mouth for the zic-zac bird to enter and pick his teeth.

The natives go after their food in an equally leisurely way. I have seen an old man stop at intervals along a river bank and stick a fish pole into the ground, bend it over and set it on a trigger with the hook well in the water. Too lazy to stay and watch his lines, he went home. In the evening he returned to take the fish which, having nibbled the bait, had set off the trigger and been yanked out of the water to hang on the hook until collection time.

One evening my coolies got supper by wading into a small pond. They stirred up the mud so that the fish had to come to the surface for a breath of good air. Then they skewered the unsuspecting prey with large knives.

Another day I saw a young boy take some twenty little fish rods and go out into the shallow waters of his father's rice fields. Setting the rods, one by one, in various parts of the field so that the hooks dangled in the water, he doubled back to the first little pole and took off a three-inch fish. In no time he had what he considered to be a good catch, about a hundred, and started home. With a grin on his face he took one of them and rubbed it on the ground. As he held it in his hand the fish puffed up like a ball from the gulps of air it began to swallow. When it was blown up hard the youngster bounced it like a rubber ball and finally threw it into the water where it collapsed to normal size and swam away. It was a Malay puffing fish. To top off the afternoon, the boy brought out a little two-inch fish which he kept in a bottle. He called a friend who had a similar fish and challenged the latter's pet to a fight. A crowd collected. When bets had been made, my boy's fish went into the other's bottle, and the fight was on. Scales were the only things to be seen for some time. Finally one of the fish sank dead to the bottom of the bottle. My boy's entrant had won in what is a national Malayan pastime.

Well, that was topsy-turvy Malay. While there I wanted to get back to rightside-up civilization, but now I want to see that queer land once more before I die.

A Robin Shows the Way

CHAPTER TWO

MY experiences in Malaya left me an invalid, broken physically, financially and almost mentally. I looked like a skeleton and felt like one. The six most interesting years of my life were over. Doctors in Malay hospitals sent me home to die. But I did not even have a home to die in. Some quirk in my fever-racked brain suggested America and so they sent me to San Francisco.

I arrived there in 1918 and wondered whether I would have enough money for my burial. Such funereal thoughts, despite my pernicious anæmia and sprue (a disease caused by a fungus), were soon driven from my mind. The sight of white people moving about in an orderly pattern; the realization that I was no longer to face the jungle and watch it stretch its leafy tentacles toward me like a giant octopus of the plant world seeking to engulf me, gave me renewed vigor. I shambled into the Saint

Francis Hotel and ordered tea. While I drank I feasted my eyes on the men and women about me, not with envy but because I was able to be there and see them. I made up my mind to remain on this earth and boarded a train for Portland, Oregon, where my brother lived.

The reason for my move was simple. The London School of Tropical Medicine had advised me to live on a diet of liver and strawberries, supplemented with tripe, brains and the general interior furnishings of animals. My brother had been educated in England as a surgeon, but when he fainted at the sight of blood at his first operation, my father sent him to America where he became a successful butcher. In him I saw the provider of the major portion of my diet.

Then, too, arrival in Portland would complete my first circumnavigation of the globe. After my graduation from the University of London as a civil engineer I went to practice my profession in the wilds of Saskatchewan on the survey of the Grand Trunk Pacific Railway where I contracted typhoid fever and was invalided to Portland. There was nothing for a civil engineer to do when I recovered and so I became a private detective in the employ of one of the city's largest department stores.

My first job was to test the honesty of a certain

red-haired sales girl. I was given twenty dollars and instructed to buy a pair of shoes from her, to have them wrapped and to get a bill with her number on it. As an afterthought, according to my instructions, I was to pick up a pair of laces, ask the price, pay her, put them in my pocket and walk out. If she took the money without giving me a bill, she would be accused of stealing and I would make my first catch as a detective.

Everything worked fine. I bought the shoes, picked up the laces and handed her ten cents. When she pocketed the money and smiled a sweet good-by something compelled me to say: "You'd better give me a bill for those laces, Miss, I'm a detective." That night the store paid me four dollars salary and fired me.

I decided to go back to civil engineering and taught that subject at my alma mater in London. My professorial duties palled on me after two years and wishing something dangerous to do, I set out, as I have already related, for Malaya.

Great were the changes which had taken place in Portland since my detective experience. The city was busily building ships and an 8,000-ton, fabricated steamer was being launched every five days. For several months my brother most hospitably furnished my diet and when I regained my strength I presented myself at the offices of the Northwest Steel Shipyard to ask for an engineering job.

"Nothing doing," said a pimply youth. "Give you a job as a tracer at $60 a month."

I spurned his offer, took off my white collar, bought a pair of overalls with the slogan "You Can't Bust 'Em" sewed into the garment, and within an hour I was back at the same shipyard on a laborer's job at seven dollars a day. I wandered about the place for six hours with nothing to do when a cheerful-looking youth approached me.

"Say, kid," he said, "do you want a partner?"

"That's exactly what I want," I replied.

"O. K., let's go to the tool house."

From the look of my partner and the number of his acquaintances, he evidently was an old hand at the game and I was delighted at my luck.

Together we climbed down an inviting-looking manhole dragging into the hold of a new ship a sack of tools. The warmth was welcome and made me think of the jungle I had so recently left. We crawled along amid the terrific din of pneumatic hammers and dodged showers of red hot sparks until we arrived at a cozy little corner where the light came in dimly through a number of rivet holes. Flinging his sack down my partner turned to me.

"Watch the tools," he said, and disappeared in the gloom. Two hours later he returned.

"Now, I'll watch them," he announced.

For two days we watched one another's tools until a foreman shouted down the hole for men. I was put on a gang of bolters-up. Only those who have spent long years in the tropics will understand what I suffered working in cold rain, filthy, sworn at, hustled about and slave-driven. It was a contrast from being a sahib in Malaya with many servants to care for my wants. Now I was a "coolie" myself, and I wondered what my Malay servants would have thought of their mighty master's low estate.

When I could no longer bear the cold and exposure, I tried a heater's job, warming up rivets in a furnace and throwing them fifty or sixty feet to a riveter. Then I was made the catcher with a ridiculously little tin can to snare red hot rivets thrown at me. Occasionally I caught one but by the time I handed it to the riveter it was too cold and I was reduced from catcher to bucker-up.

Holding a heavy piece of iron against a rivet while the riveter hammers it with a pneumatic hammer was no easy task for me. I was continually vibrated backward and forward, and when I got home the first night I still vibrated. That finished me and the foreman suggested getting into the mold loft where the ship is drawn.

I had no idea that ships were drawn full size and not sketched on drawing boards. Wooden patterns are nailed over the huge drawings and from them various parts of the ship are reproduced in iron. Although drawing on the floor made one susceptible to housemaid's knee, the thought of working under cover attracted me and into the mold loft I went.

One day while busily drawing on the floor, I bumped head on into another man.

"I beg your pardon," he exclaimed politely. His drawing-room manner surprised me and I discovered that he was Robert Bruce Horsfall, the bird artist, who later became art editor of Nature Magazine and accompanied William Beebe into the jungles of Malaya. His painted backgrounds may now be seen in the American Museum of Natural History.

"People are more interested in ships than birds nowadays," he told me, "so I am drawing ships for a living."

My mold loft career was brief. One night my finger slipped into the planing machine and the end was cut off slice by slice. I received free medical treatment at the shipyard hospital consisting of a liberal supply of talcum powder on the wound and some bandages. Then I was awarded seven dollars compensation and fired.

Again I was broke.

But my health was better and my spirits on the upgrade. Into the Portland Public Library I wandered and seeing notice of a free meeting of the Oregon Audubon Society, I decided to attend. At that time I knew nothing of Audubon and was entirely unprepared for a lecture on birds.

"This is a robin," said a man on the platform as I entered the room. He was holding up a bird the size of a chicken with a brownish red breast.

"That's not a robin; it's a thrush," I spoke up.

Everybody's neck stretched at this.

"It *is* a robin!" insisted the speaker.

"Well," I replied, "I never saw a robin like that before. Robins have red breasts, not brown and they never grow to the size of the one you have there. Besides there never were any robins in America until the Fathers of the Mayflower came here. When they got lonesome for their English robins, they dubbed the American thrush a robin."

"Now that you've spoiled my lecture," said the irate speaker ironically, "how would you like to come up on the platform and tell us what you know about birds."

The audience was distinctly hostile and so was I.

But the chance was too good to miss and I accepted the speaker's challenge.

I told a few stories of my experiences in the Malay jungle, of birds that slept upside down and of animals that can fly. As I went on the expressions on the faces in the audience gradually changed from interest to contemptuous incredulity. The more incredulous they became the more I told. Finally I said:

"Did you ever hear of a hornbill? This is one of the most famous Malayan birds. It has black and white feathers, and boasts of a beak a foot long. The bird itself is about five feet long. When the female is ready to lay an egg she goes to a hollow tree and gets inside. The male then collects mud in his beak and plasters his wife into the tree so that she cannot get out. He leaves a small hole through which she can stick her beak. There she stays for about two and a half months. As a rule the hornbill lays one or sometimes two eggs and while she is sitting, she loses all her feathers, even her wing and tail feathers, and grows a new supply."

At this there was a stir in the audience as several persons prepared to walk out, but before they had time to leave the room I added:

"All the time the hornbill is sitting, her husband feeds her on strychnine."

Then I added: "I know lots of men who would like to do the same."

That was the last straw. The meeting broke up and I went home to dine on grapenuts. A day or so later the director of the Oregon Audubon Society called upon me to say he had checked my hornbill story and had found my statements to be correct. Whereupon he invited me to give another lecture for the society the following Saturday—free.

"What am I to do between now and Saturday?" I asked politely, my mind on my last four dollars in the world.

"Aren't you a lecturer?" the director inquired.

"Heavens, no," I said.

"Then you ought to be," he replied.

Thinking of my injured hand and the impossibility of practicing my engineering profession, I asked how one got lecture engagements.

"Go to the churches in town and offer to talk on the jungle," the director suggested.

I took his advice. I visited church after church. No one wanted me until I came to a Methodist church where the genial pastor listened to my story and said he was having a meeting of the Epworth League on Friday.

"What is the Epworth League," I asked.

"The Epworth League," he replied, "is a society

which has supper in the basement of the church and talks about it afterward. Next Friday is Father and Son night and we expect a large crowd. How about you speaking on the jungle and then taking half of the silver collection?"

"Marvelous!" I replied, anticipating a free dinner with a silver collection for dessert.

Friday came. The lecture hall was crowded. The 500 people were delighted with my talk and the parson congratulated me on drawing the largest crowd they ever had. Then the silver collection was taken up and I got half of seven dollars.

That night I faced the greatest problem of my life.

I had seen for myself that even though the collection amounted to only seven dollars, I had the ability to hold the attention of a large audience. What should I do? I had spent fifteen years acquiring an engineering education. I had university degrees, diplomas, certificates, prizes and a real love for my profession. I had put in nine years in actual practice and had written a book on surveying and astronomy. Now, despite all of my education and experience, the best I could do was a laborer's job in a shipyard.

I decided to talk for a living.

Within two weeks I addressed the Oregon Society

of Engineers. I was the guest of honor at a banquet and sat beside the president of the Northwest Steel Shipyard who had no inkling whatever that he was listening to one of his own laborers.

Thus it was that I made an important discovery about my profession—i.e.: it is much more profitable to talk about engineering than to practice it!

Talking for a Living

CHAPTER THREE

ADVENTURE is an event, according to Webster's dictionary, the issue of which is determined by chance. From that moment in Portland when I took a chance and decided that henceforth I no longer was an engineer but a lecturer and explorer, my life has been a series of adventures.

The idea that to have an adventure one must be in some great danger is quite wrong. For example:

While surveying in the Malay jungle, it was my custom to have a series of camps erected at intervals of about six miles in the general direction of any survey. Each camp consisted of a house 15 feet square perched on piles, a kitchen, a small shack for my cook and boy and a little bathhouse. While the cook's quarters and the kitchen usually were behind my house, the bathhouse rarely was in the same place twice running, its situation usually being determined by the water supply.

Each day we would proceed with the survey, cutting our way further and further ahead through dense vegetation. When work was over we would retrace our steps along the cutting back to camp. Eventually the time would come when the new camp would be nearer than the old. One day, when we had stopped work later than usual, I decided to find the new camp. It was dark when we arrived. The whole place looked strange but I was dead tired and did not inspect the building. Turning into bed I slept soundly until about 2 o'clock in the morning when the trumpeting of elephants waked me. I sprang up and listened. Sure enough a herd of them was quite close by, so close that every now and then I could hear their stomachs rumbling as they digested their supper.

Suddenly the animals began crashing through the undergrowth. Knowing that elephants have a decided objection to anything unusual in the jungle, especially houses, I had visions of them finding and destroying my camp. By this time I was trembling with excitement and snatching up my revolver I rushed to the veranda. My heart pounded as I saw a huge black object that seemed to be contemplating the house, undecided whether to push it over or to leave it unmolested. I was taking no chances and quickly emptied all five chambers of the revolver at it.

Nothing happened—I had shot the bathhouse!

Now that was a real adventure although there had been no danger. For what does it matter if a man experiences all the thrill of being in a dangerous situation and upon investigation finds the danger gone?

There can be adventure even in vaudeville. Consider my first one after several lectures in Portland.

I was appearing five times a day at the old Lyric Theater in that city. The management featured me as the "Jungleman." I used to stand outside the theater and listen to patrons in front of the posters arguing whether I was white or a half-cast negro.

My act lasted eight minutes. I would make my entrance to the strains of a waltz which gradually faded away as I began telling my jungle tales. The climax was a demonstration with costumes of how Malay girls dressed and undressed without undressing. Some of the brilliantly colored clothes were those in which I slept in Malaya while others were from my collection of native sarongs.

While I was waiting in the wings for my turn on the afternoon of Friday, which was pay day, a Western Union boy handed me a message. It read that if I wanted a long contract I would have to leave the theater at once because the manager with the offer was waiting in the lobby and had to catch a train.

I was due on the stage in less than two minutes. Should I go on when my waltz began or should I take a chance, miss my act, sign the new contract and trust to luck that the management would allow me to make my appearance out of turn?

No one ever needed his $85 salary more than I did but here was a chance for a long-term contract instead of a week's engagement. The actors begged me not to leave the theater saying that the manager would only be too delighted to hold out my salary for breach of contract. The orchestra started to play my waltz. I decided to take the chance. Instead of walking on the stage I ran into the lobby. I could hear the musicians playing my waltz over and over again. "Sign here," said the visiting manager. I signed. The contract was for a Chautauqua engagement.

When the famous "Jungleman" did not appear several persons got up and demanded their money back. As they stormed the box office the manager of the theater rushed up and implored me to go on out of turn.

"What about my $85?" I asked.

"Okay," he said, "get back to the stage right away."

ADVENTURE!

I was able to catch the 15th rendition of my waltz and when I appeared before the footlights I received an ovation of cheers.

Unlike vaudeville Chautauqua programs always opened with prayer and the most successful speakers were those who, like William Jennings Bryan, took for their themes "Mother, Home and Heaven."

I started in Canada where I lectured twice a day in 120 towns in 120 days, and slept in 120 different beds. Some of these were fitted with blankets nailed to the footboard.

The conditions under which we lectured were by no means ideal. In the afternoon the seats were half-filled with restless children and squalling babies. Now and then a dog or a cat would walk on the stage or start a fight. The speaker would look down on a sea of perspiring faces, chewing gum, cracking nuts, sucking candy or absorbing ice cream cones. On many occasions we had to contend with disturbances unseen by the audience as I did when traveling with a menagerie called Pamahasika's Pets. Mr. Pamahasika's pets went on at night and were housed under the platform from which I lectured during the afternoon. The cats, dogs, ponies and monkeys combined vocal efforts to howl me down every time I took a step.

One day I lectured in Watrous, Canada. The tent

was pitched on the open prairie and was packed with farmers and their wives, many of whom had driven 70 miles to attend the meeting. The tent, a particularly large one, was raised on two ordinary telegraph poles.

When I started speaking I thought the air was ominously still. Suddenly, without the slightest warning, the lights went out and the whole tent including the telegraph poles ascended to heaven and vanished. A terrific tornado had sucked the tent up into the sky. Rain came down in torrents, children screamed, women fainted and dozens of persons were blown down and rolled over and over in the black mud. The tent never was seen again but the telegraph poles came to earth a quarter mile away.

The Pullman and all its comforts did not exist so far as we Chautauqua people were concerned. We traveled in day coaches night and day. By early morning the men usually had removed their shoes and collars while women lolled sleepily with their hair disheveled and blouses open. Fretful children would eat bananas and fight for paper cups in an atmosphere you could cut with a knife. Yet the unfortunate "talent" were expected to arrive in each town, happy and smiling.

William Jennings Bryan could sleep through it all. The first time I saw him he was lying on the floor of a little wayside railway station sound asleep and huddled up in his overcoat. At 4 a. m., when the train arrived, he waked, found a seat in the day coach and within five minutes was sound asleep again.

Some of the most amusing adventures that ever befell me in America came while I toured the country lecturing on Malaya under my own management. I would buy a railway ticket to a little town which had an American plan hotel and I would often arrive broke. Here I would stay without having to pay a cent for board and lodging until the end of the week. By that time I had looked over the town and made friends with the local school authorities, parsons and theater managers.

By day I would give free lectures in the public schools in return for permission to announce that my remarkable jungle lecture would be given in the local theater at the end of the week. Usually I took the theater on a percentage basis, paying the manager 40 per cent of the receipts.

When the great night of the show arrived, provided there was fine weather, the theater would be packed with large family parties. Children were always my best friends and they insisted on dragging parents and relatives to see the pictures which illustrated the free talks I gave in the schools.

ADVENTURE!

After the show I would pay my hotel bill and buy a ticket to the next town along the main line.

One cold night in the middle of January, I landed in a small Western town whose hotel had the usual rocking chairs, each accompanied by a cuspidor, placed in a row in the front window. Outside it was below zero but inside one nearly roasted because of the large anthracite coal stove in the lobby around which there congregated nightly town characters who squirted streams of tobacco juice alternately at the stovepipe and floor.

The only warm bedroom in the place was the one through which the stovepipe ran. Others varied in temperature as their distance from the pipe. In each of these rooms was a bowl and pitcher.

On this occasion I was called at 3 o'clock in the morning to catch a train. As I made my way along the deserted main street to the depot I noticed another man following me. He was carrying a very bulky object under his long winter coat. The snow under foot squeaked and as I breathed through my nostrils my breath seemed to freeze going in, and to fall on my coat like snow when it came out.

On reaching the railroad platform I saw the stranger take from under his coat one of the hotel's bedroom pitchers. He dashed it on the ground where it broke into a hundred pieces and went down on his hands and knees apparently looking for something.

I asked him what he had lost.

"My teeth," he mumbled.

When he had retired for the night he had placed his false teeth in the pitcher of water and waking at 3 a. m. had found the water in the pitcher solidly frozen with his teeth imprisoned.

Another time I had been engaged to give a humorous lecture in a small New Hampshire town. The hall in which I spoke was extremely small and was packed to the doors. Sitting in the front row were two men dressed in black frock coats who annoyed me by continually looking at their watches.

When my lecture was over, every one left the hall but the two frock-coated gentlemen who continued to consult their watches while I packed my paraphernalia.

"What's on your mind?" I asked petulantly. "The show's over and I shall be here only 10 more minutes. What are you waiting for?"

"Well," said one of them, rather mournfully, "we have a 'stiff' in the back room and we need your table to lay it out."

I had delivered my humorous talk in the local undertaking parlor within six feet of a corpse.

Romance in Rainbow Isle

CHAPTER FOUR

MY lectures on the Malay jungle were a huge success and they enabled me to barnstorm my way across the continent from Vancouver to Boston. After some weeks on the Atlantic Coast I realized that if lecturing was to remain my profession I had to acquire new material. And so I went to Bermuda.

It was not by mere chance that I chose that group of islands. My father came from there and when I left New York I took with me indelible childish impressions of their beauty as well as stories of pirates and pioneers my father had told me. There was a romance, too. He did his best to keep it a secret but I got an inkling of it through postcards which came to him from Bermuda on his birthdays and at Christmas with the message: "Love from Nattie." I remembered that mother used to ask who Nattie was but there never was an answer. Father would smile and tuck the card away in his pocket.

ADVENTURE!

For more than 30 years those cards had come from Nattie before I ever saw one, and they continued to arrive regularly twice a year until my father died at 83.

My father lived in Bermuda at the outbreak of the American Civil War when it was headquarters for ships that ran the blockade and supplied cotton to the North and gunpowder to the South. As a Bermudian his sympathies were with the South, especially Virginia. That is traceable, perhaps, to the fact that some of the hardy Englishmen who discovered Bermuda later became Virginians.

My father was a clerk in the government dock-yard in St. George's and it was his duty to pay weekly wages to the laborers. He was handing out the pay envelopes one day when a negro, a Northern sympathizer, threw a brick at the paymaster and struck my father behind the ear fracturing his skull.

After lying insensible for many days, he was placed on board a sailing vessel and sent home to England where he remained unconscious in Devonport Hospital. One day a doctor, who thought he was original, said:

"Let's cut out a piece of his skull to see what happens."

This surgeon evidently did not know that far back in the Stone Age, people used to do the same operation with a flint knife to cure headaches. Such an amazing operation attracted wide attention and in the presence of 30 leading surgeons the operation of trepanning was performed. A circular section of the skull, the size of a 25-cent piece, was removed and almost immediately the patient opened his eyes. When he discovered he was in England he was amazed and demanded that he be sent back to Bermuda immediately.

"Young man," the surgeon said, "my advice to you is to forget Bermuda. You will probably die at any minute. You had better draw out your government pension in a lump sum."

Father took his advice and blew in all the money immediately. But instead of dying, he lived far longer than all the doctors who predicted his imminent end.

When he found he was not going to die, he married a girl he saw through the camera obscura on Plymouth Hoe. This was a giant periscope constructed underground. The great thrill was to go below and look at the reflection of the people walking about on the surface above. In due time my father became the breadwinner for eight healthy children of which brood I was the baby.

That I should learn anything of my father's past and his Nattie was furthest from my mind while collecting material and taking motion pictures in Bermuda. One day I happened upon a lovely colonial house with a beautiful, old-fashioned garden. Something inside me seemed to say:

"Enter that gate; go up to the house; you will be welcome."

I entered the gate and as I walked up the drive I met an elderly woman with white hair. I apologized for my intrusion.

"I am most anxious to take a few photographs of your lovely old house, may I?"

"Why, certainly you may," she answered.

As I started for the house she called:

"Just a minute. Would you mind telling me your name?"

"My name," I said, surprised, "is Wells."

"Wells? Is it possible that your name also is Grant?" she asked in a strange tone.

"It certainly is," I confessed. "I'm Grant Carveth Wells, but I rarely use the Grant."

Then it flashed upon me.

"Is it possible," I asked, "that you are . . . Nattie?"

"No," she said. "Nattie is dead. So you are Grant's son. She died soon after news of your father's death. I am her sister."

Then, taking me by the arm, she led me into the

house and showed me two pictures. One was a portrait of a young man with Dundreary whiskers—Father. The other was a portrait of a very pretty young girl dressed in a crinoline—Nattie.

Nattie's sister pointed to some old dust-covered bows and arrows propped in a corner of the room.

"That was your father's bow and the smaller one was Nattie's," she told me. "They often used to shoot on the lawn."

What a romance was gradually unfolded to me! Did my father know the depth of Nattie's love for him? The accident that caused his return to England in an unconscious condition; his ultimate discovery that he was doomed to a life of uncertainty with sudden death always lurking in the background, probably determined him never to return to Bermuda. Then along came the other girl and a large family to support. Bermuda became a dream, a physical impossibility, for those were the days of sailing ships when a journey to the islands was not undertaken lightly, nor without great expense.

But Nattie never forgot. She remained faithful to him and died unmarried.

During the course of my stay in Bermuda I rented the top story of an old coral house named "Cedarhurst" where I met with another surprise. The occupant of the ground floor was an elderly lady who seemed lonely. On Christmas Day I paid her a visit and when I mentioned my name she exclaimed:

"Why, you must be the son of my old friend Grant Wells. . . . I am Mrs. Butterfield, and my husband was the surgeon who treated your father when he was so badly injured. This is the very room into which your father was carried. Why, I used to dance with Grant Wells."

I must say that Grant proved to have been a very popular young man to judge from what Mrs. Butterfield and other old ladies told me of the girls he used to dance with. One day I thought I'd try to get a man's point of view by questioning an elderly Bermudian.

"Did you know my father, Grant Wells?" I asked.

"I certainly did," he replied in a flash. "He was a regular devil."

Just as he said that his sister came up. Looking me over she laughed and added:

"And you are exactly like your father."

While on a visit to Ireland Island, the Bermuda naval station, I found that my grandmother had been matron of the hospital and that her maiden name was Dalzell, Sally Dalzell. I also discovered that Dalzell is the family name of the Earls of Carnwath and that I am a blue-blooded aristocrat.

Dalzell means "I dare" and so far as I could

ascertain the name originated in the Middle Ages when the son of the Earl of Carnwath volunteered to rescue a fair maiden who was imprisoned in a castle surrounded by a deep moat. In order to rescue her, he had to take off his armor, swim naked to the castle, grab the girl and swim back again. This romantic feat explains the presence of the naked men on the coat of arms of the Earls of Carnwath.

Close to Ireland Island, I found Somerset Church where most of my uncles and aunts and other relatives for generations were baptized. The sexton offered to show me the very seat where my father sat.

"It was right there," he said, indicating a comfortable corner seat in the front row. "But your father always was a-looking backwards."

"Why was that?" I asked.

"Nattie used to sit in the gallery, sir," he replied.

If people say as sweet things about me when I have gone as they still say about my romantic father, I shall not be unhappy.

It is possible that some of my ancestors trace their blood back to those who set out with Sir George Somers, admiral of the "Sea Venture," which, with eight other ships, started for Virginia in 1609. Aboard the boats were 500 British colonists and two English gentlemen—the gallant Captain Christopher Newport and the noble Sir Thomas Gates, newly appointed Governor of Virginia. During a storm the "Sea Venture" was separated from the other ships and wrecked on an island which the admiralty map distinctly showed was "inhabited by devils." Instead of devils they found hundreds of pigs and remained in what is now known as Bermuda until new ships could be built for the trip to Virginia.

A year after he left England, Admiral Somers sailed up the James River to find to his great surprise that coming downstream was another sailing ship with 60 persons aboard. These were the survivors of the 440 colonists who had reached Jamestown in safety only to be attacked by Indians and sickness. They were now leaving Virginia.

The admiral persuaded them to turn back and back they went to recolonize that famous little town several years before the Mayflower left England. The great problem was food. Once more Admiral Somers saved the day by revisiting Bermuda in order to secure a cargo of pork. Upon his safe arrival in the "devil" islands, he celebrated with a huge roast pork banquet from which he contracted indigestion and died.

It so happened that the admiral had with him in Bermuda the heirs to his English estates and like most heirs they were eager to return home to take over the old gentleman's property. They needed proof of his death to take with them. Poor Admiral Somers, however, had loved Bermuda and had expressed a wish to remain there. Finally a compromise was agreed upon. The admiral's heart was removed and buried in Bermuda while the rest of him was taken to England, and upon his arrival there was no doubt that he was dead and the heirs came into their inheritance.

The romantic return of the Virginia colonists to London caused a sensation. They had a story to tell and they told it so well that, as was to be expected, a real estate company was formed to divide Bermuda into lots. What was needed was publicity and an enterprising real estate promoter inspired a popular writer of the day, William Shakespeare, to write "The Tempest."

In no time Shakespeare's book became a best seller. Every one began talking of Bermuda. Money poured into the coffers of the new company and with this a sailing ship was built on which 60 people left to colonize in the name of England the Somers Islands, better known as "Ye Faire Bermoothes."

For those who can't afford the far-off places, I can think of no better spot for adventure than Bermuda. Vessels of every description are always arriving off the very reef upon which the "Sea Venture" was wrecked, to await the pilot. As soon as he comes aboard, the ship threads her way through the dangerous waters of the north shore past cedar-covered islets. Here and there you may see a suspicious looking vessel—a rum runner. But it is just as well not to jump to conclusions. The first rum runner I saw turned out to be the private yacht of Mr. Vanderbilt.

After about an hour's sailing, your ship, accompanied by dinghies, reaches Hamilton, capital of Bermuda.

Sailing a Bermuda dinghy is an adventure in itself. While one man handles the boat, three men bail it out!

Before tying up alongside the main street of the town, your attention will be drawn to White's Island, which Britain gave to the United States for a naval station during the World War. When the armistice was signed this tiny piece of the British Empire was returned by the United States with great formality.

When you land you will notice the prevalence of British uniforms. Upon the cuffs of policemen are the detachable bands worn by British guardians of the law the world over to remind them that they are on duty!

ADVENTURE!

Evidence of Bermuda economy is seen on every side. For instance, notice that old two-story building with an enormous rubber tree in front. That is the combined Public Library and Natural History Museum. Probably one out of every thousand visitors enters it, yet a visit is well worth while because the diminutive museum contains the finest collection of prehistoric eggs in the world. Really old ones, of course. Unlike those found in the Gobi Desert, Bermuda's eggs are not of dinosaurs but of birds about the size of the ordinary hen variety. They are found embedded in the soft coral.

Sixty per cent of Bermudians are black in color: that is to say sixty per cent of the population—not of the individuals! They speak the perfect English of their old owners and bear their names as well. On Sundays and festivals, the men go to church dressed in frock coats and top hats, while the women usually dress in white muslin. Most of them belong to various lodges and they often appear on Sundays garbed in all their regalia. On one occasion I saw a procession of men dressed in the height of Bond Street fashion carrying pickaxes, shovels and a large basket of bricks!

The best way to see Bermuda is to rent a boat and watch the rainbows play. Mine was the "Julia" and her captain was Samson, a negro as black as ink.

ADVENTURE!

One day, Samson suggested a sail to Tucker's Island.

"What's there?" I enquired.

"Just a hole, sir," he replied.

That's a queer thing about Bermuda. The principal sights are holes of one kind or another. This one was Tucker's Hole. It turned out to be just a small limestone cavern containing immense stalactites and stalagmites. The latter were under water, which is evidence that Bermuda is slowly sinking into the sea.

Noticing my interest in them, Samson explained, pointing to the roof of the cave:

"Them on the roof are called 'tites,' and them under the water are called 'mites'! The tites are coming down and the mites are going up and when the mites meet the tites, they'll be mighty tight!"

If you want a real adventure just go shell hunting. Sooner or later you will have an encounter with an octopus. One of the horrible-looking monsters seized me by the wrist while I had my hand in the water. I yelled for Samson who ran up with a boat hook. After a few moments he had the octopus out on dry land. While I was photographing the creature, it squirted a stream of India ink all over my white ducks. In disgust I pushed the devil back into the sea where it immediately turned from red to green and darted away with amazing speed.

The idea that an octopus is sluggish in its movements is wrong. An octopus can dart about like lightning and often leaps out of the water when chasing its prey. Incidentally, should you ever be caught in the toils of an octopus, the best thing to do is to turn the animal inside out.

From Tucker's Island we sailed to Admiralty Cove, the private harbor of the Admiral of Bermuda. On the other end of the jetty stands the famous statue of Neptune, famous because no one knows anything about it! Opposite Neptune is a great cliff of coral from which the Australian swimmer, Annette Kellerman, dived. By the way, when the same Australian lady dived into one of the glass tanks at the Bermuda Aquarium, she went clear through the plate glass and landed on the floor in a mess of fish.

On the way home we sailed past an immense floating dock, large enough to hold a man-o'-war. It was made in England and towed across the Atlantic. Before its arrival in Bermuda, an enormous hole had to be excavated to receive it because floating docks need large holes into which they sink. When

ADVENTURE!

Bermudian laborers digging this particular hole reached a depth of 30 feet, they were astonished to find cedar trees in fairly good condition—more evidence that the islands are slowly subsiding.

A *Migration to Atlantis*

CHAPTER FIVE

HAVE you ever heard of a lemming or lemmus, as it is known to zoölogists? I hadn't either until I started for Lapland. It is a little animal about the size of a small rat, and is one of nature's greatest mysteries. Its bones have been found in the caves of prehistoric man. Lemmings live today but no naturalist has been able to find even one except during migrations. Then millions of them appear, moving slowly to the sea, laying waste the land they traverse.

They move through fire and water, down precipices, over almost impassable obstacles until they reach the ocean. Once there, they swim straight out and disappear until the next migration which may be 18 or 20 years later. The legend is that they're looking for the lost Continent of Atlantis.

Scientists maintain that the swimming out to sea is a case of inherited instinct; that they're looking for land which once was there, but has sunk beneath the water.

Julian Huxley, the biologist, has checked lemming migrations as far back as there is any record. He advances the theory that there is some connection between the migrations and sun spots. Every year there has been a lemming migration he has found there has been unusual activity in the sun. And it very well may be that their propagation is affected by certain rays.

The story of this little animal fascinated me and when I promised Dr. F. A. Lucas, honorary director of the American Museum of Natural History, that I would bring a few of these creatures back with me, I never dreamed that within six weeks I should witness one of their migrations. The purpose of our expedition, which was headed by Dr. Clyde Fisher, curator of education at the museum, was to study the Lapps during the Summer, when they follow the reindeer. Through the Swedish Government we obtained the services of Dr. Bergstrom, one of the greatest authorities on the nomadic peoples of Lapland.

It was midnight and the sun still shining brightly on the lake when our party, invited to accompany Tuolja, the Lapp, and his family on their annual summer journey to the mountains, reached the base of Stora Sjolfallet, the highest waterfall in Lapland. The water was going over green, tumbling vertically about ninety feet, and in the mist above was a wonderful rainbow. In order to avoid the fall and reach the upper level of the lake beyond it, we portaged our boats for about a mile. And the first thing I observed was the dead body of a little animal as large as a rat. It was a lemming.

Earlier in the day a snowy owl, perched on a rock near the shore, had warned us by his presence that the lemmings were coming. This species of owl and other birds and animals seem to know when there is a migration. They come in droves from other countries and when the migration is at an end, they're left stranded without any food. After the 1924 migration, hundreds of snowy owls flew across to Canada where they were almost unknown.

As I was clambering over great, rounded bowlders covered with moss and lichen, sometimes sinking almost to my knees in the thick, velvety blanket of moss and dwarf birch, I was attracted by a strange little noise. It was something like the bark of a lapdog—a cross between a whine and a complaining bark. Then, close to my feet, sitting up on its hind legs and showing its teeth, I saw my first live lemming. I was so excited that I shouted for my motion picture camera and took reels of film, in case this might be the only specimen in Lapland!

It was a pretty animal, very much like a medium-sized guinea pig. Its fur was a rich golden brown with gray under the jaws and neck. Evidently this lemming was very angry, because it jumped up at my legs, snapped and snarled and furiously attacked me. When I retreated a few paces it calmed down. It then began to eat some heather and took no further notice of me.

When Tuolja and Fisher arrived it began to attack each of us in turn, barking, fighting and sometimes jumping two feet in the air. At the end of the scrimmage, however, I caught the little animal alive by persuading him to jump into my hat, whence I transferred him into Dr. Fisher's camera case. To give him something to chew on before going to bed, I provided him with about twice his own weight of grass. But just as I dropped off to sleep he waked me with a scratching sound. The little gourmand had eaten all the grass and most of the camera case's velvet lining.

Next day, as our journey continued, we came upon a sight I shall never forget. Lemmings were everywhere. They covered a strip of Lapland at least twenty miles wide. There must have been at least some three hundred millions in all. I had always pictured a lemming migration as a vast swarm of animals packed closely together. Instead I found that each claimed as its preserve an area measuring about ten feet by ten. Left alone, the animal would remain motionless, except for the movement of the jaws while eating. But as there was constant trespassing, and since a lemming has a highly developed sense of proprietorship, there were always plenty of fights.

"Where do they all come from?" I asked Tuolja.

"From heaven," he replied, pointing to the sky.

"Where do they go?"

This Tuolja did not know. All he could tell was that these animals suddenly appear and eat their way slowly across country to the lowlands. Highest mountains and widest lakes are no obstacles.

Their droppings form deposits so thick on the mountain snows and glaciers that the streams flowing down become polluted. A lemming migration is usually accompanied by an outbreak of lemming fever. The natives build huge fires and thousands of the little beasts die but the rest move right on.

They inflict tremendous damage. They devastate the food lands of the reindeer and force that animal to become carnivorous. The deer, Tuolja said, step on the lemmings and bite off their heads. They eat the latter and leave the bodies.

On land they are remarkably tenacious of life and they are so prolific that nothing can stop them. They have two or three litters of young during a migration period with from five to seven in a litter. The young will breed the same season and you can see that it does not take long for a pair of lemmings to raise quite a family. This overpopulation, according to scientists, causes starvation. Whereupon the animals desert their homes for new pastures.

Eventually, sometimes after a steady journey of two years, they reach the sea. Here they crowd into a great mass and when one is pushed into the water, he begins to swim. Blindly the others follow the leader and swim away to destruction.

I know it is strange that they should swim out to sea when they swim so poorly, but they do. They do not have webbed feet and they are one of the few animals in the world that have hair on the bottoms of the feet.

Sir Wilfred T. Grenfell, the medical missionary of Newfoundland and Labrador, who has observed lemming migrations, discovered that the splash of an oar will drown one of them when it is swimming and so will a heavy sea. Yet some of them must survive because they continue to migrate but where and how, no one knows. Every Lapp or Swedish student will tell you that at the end of a migration not a single lemming will be seen for many years until suddenly millions of them appear again, seemingly from nowhere.

At Home with Santa Claus

CHAPTER SIX

S ANTA CLAUS is a Lapp.
Until I went upon my expedition to Lapland,
I had seriously doubted his very existence. But now,
thank heaven, I know that in spite of jazz, joy-rides
and grape juice, he lives happily in Lapland. Not
always, however, does he ride over the snow and
ice in a sled drawn by reindeer. One summer I
found him sitting on a river bank in the midst of
violets and forget-me-nots, whisking away arctic
mosquitoes as he fished for salmon trout.

Santa Claus lives under the protection of the
Swedish Government which makes no attempt
whatever to change his mode of living. His children get a simple education sufficient for their
needs, not in Swedish schools but in nomad Lapp
schools which accompany the Claus tribes from
place to place as they follow their reindeer.

For hundreds of years these reindeer have migrated to the highlands of Lapland every Spring, returning to the wooded lowlands in the Fall. And the Lapps always have followed them, keeping so closely to the same route in the annual hegira that the same fireplaces are used year after year and one encampment becomes as much a home as another. Lapps, therefore, continually experience the joys of homecoming. Were it not for a certain kind of lichen which the Lapps call reindeer-moss, there probably would be no Lapps in Lapland. For this lichen is as essential to reindeer as the reindeer is to the Lapps. Lapps live on reindeer, and the reindeer live on lichen.

The extreme importance the Lapp attaches to his reindeer is indicated by the fact that there are in his language more than 300 words relating to it. No one seems to know when or how these people became associated with the reindeer. Once when I questioned Johan Turi, Lapland's philosopher and wolf-hunter, he said:

"I cannot tell you where we come from, but I know this, that we Lapps always have been scared away by the approach of other people. If this had not happened, perhaps we should not have become nomads. We might have taken to building houses and living like other folks. But we fled before strangers just as the wild reindeer did. The Lapps and the reindeer ran away together. We have been companions in adversity and have lived together ever since."

Dr. Bergstrom, the Swedish government expert, had warned me never to ask a Lapp how many reindeer he had. Such a question, he said, would be as tactless as to ask an American how large a bank balance he carries. I was careful not to make the fatal error and in time Johan Turi became more talkative on the subject.

"Unto one man reindeer are food and clothing," he philosophized, "but to another, they are nothing but torment. . . . From one man and one girl they tear the sweat. Another boy and girl they freeze to death. . . . . One man they release from debt; another they bring to bankruptcy!"

Turi grew eloquent. "Man often acts toward an animal as if he had less sense than the animal. For instance, the proper load for a pack reindeer is from eighty to a hundred kilograms, but some men load him with more than he can carry, and being a dumb animal the only way in which he can make known his complaint is to lie down. Still man is so foolish that he thinks this to be unwillingness, not exhaustion, and he beats him. Some men, therefore, have not the sense to think as the reindeer thinks."

When a deer is killed most of the blood is collected in a barrel and fed to the dogs. Some of the blood is placed in the animal's stomach, after it has been removed and emptied, where it solidifies and keeps indefinitely. All meat is preserved by being smoked and dried and is eaten uncooked, being cut into thin shavings with a very sharp knife. The most prized of all parts of a reindeer are the marrow-bones, and barter for ancient marrowbones is practically the only commercial transaction carried on between Lapps. Aged marrow is as much of a delicacy to Johan Turi as Limburger cheese was to Mark Twain.

It was our good fortune to follow the reindeer with Tuolja. Just before we turned in one day (there was no night) an incident occurred which illustrates the superstitious nature of the Lapps. Musti, our chief dog, was sitting at the fire with a straw in his mouth. Tuolja, noticing the straw in the dog's mouth, exclaimed, "Ah! a guest is coming to visit us."

The words were scarcely out of his mouth when the door opened and in walked an elderly, weather-beaten Swede. Without further ceremony than the usual Lapp words of greeting, "Puorist! Puorist!" the old Swede sat down near the doorway, the place that etiquette requires a stranger to occupy until he is beckoned to a better seat by his host. After a silence of several minutes Tuolja invited the stranger to sit beside him.

Enbom, the Swede visitor, took from his pocket a cup, beautifully carved from a solid piece of birch, which he held out for coffee. He placed a lump of sugar in his mouth and slowly sipped the hot coffee through it. After lighting his pipe, Enbom produced three strangely-shaped pieces of paper, and in a few minutes he and Tuolja were in earnest conversation. While they talked, Tuolja would pick up one of the pieces of paper and closely examine it. At last he carefully cut some birch bark in the shape of a reindeer's ear. He made three V-shaped notches in the top edge and cut off the tip.

"All my reindeer have ears like that," he told the Swede. "See how different they are from the three samples you have shown me."

Dr. Bergstrom explained the mysterious confab.

"Enbom is a Government inspector of reindeer. He says that some Lapps from a near-by district have reported the loss of several deer and that he is trying to trace them."

Thus I discovered that every Lapp can identify his reindeer by marks branded or cut into their ears and that the Swedish governmental authorities keep a record of all registered reindeer ears.

"But how on earth can Tuolja know if there is a

stray in his herd of several hundred?" I asked in astonishment. I knew that reindeer are by no means the tame, domesticated animals they often are thought to be. I had seen herds gallop madly off before we could get within a quarter of a mile of them.

"He'll use his field glasses and examine the herd's ears," replied the doctor.

I remembered then that many of the Lapps I had met carried powerful field glasses, but I could not believe that even with the aid of binoculars a man could pick out one particular deer by noting the shape of its ear. Next morning, however, I saw it done. Carrying the sample ears, Tuolja and En-bom went to the top of a slight prominence, and there Tuolja began to inspect his herd through the glasses.

"Let me try, Tuolja," I requested. Although I have exceptionally good eyesight I could discern no kind of mark on the reindeers' ears. Try as I would, however, all the ears looked as alike as peas.

Tuolja laughed and took back the glasses. He surveyed the herd intently for several minutes. Suddenly he called to Enbom: "Yes, there are two strange deer and one has ears like those you are looking for."

He beckoned to the dogs which dashed away in

the direction of the deer. In a few minutes they had rounded up the herd into a compact mass. Tuolja then advanced with his lasso and roped one of the strangers. The reindeer bucked and struggled to free itself as Tuolja retrieved the rope hand over hand. When he reached the animal he unceremoniously seized it by one of its hind legs and dragged it along backwards. Not until then did I realize how very small a Lapp reindeer is. A Lapp himself is only about five feet tall, and most of the reindeer come only to his waist.

Tuolja's use of field glasses formed a sharp contrast to the method of his ancestors. In olden days, lost reindeer were located by means of a divining drum, oval in shape, measuring about eighteen inches at the larger, and twelve inches at the smaller diameter. A map of the locality was drawn upon a skin stretched across the drum. To locate a lost reindeer, the Lapp held the drum in his left hand, with the surface horizontal and level. On the map he placed a small iron ring, about an inch in diameter. He then tapped the drum with a light hammer. The blows caused the skin to vibrate so that the metal ring danced about from place to place.

Sooner or later, as the vibrations diminished or ceased altogether, the ring would settle down on the map—and there was the spot where the missing reindeer was to be sought. If it were not found, it was assumed that the animal had wandered away somewhere else. The drum was consulted again and again, until the lost animal finally was located.

So successful were the Lapps with their magic drums and other witchcraft that they unfortunately attracted the attention of that fanatical Lutheran pastor, Laestadius. Nearly a century ago this reformer rushed to Lapland and succeeded in getting the Lapps to destroy their drums, to throw away their beautiful silver ornaments and to be miserable until the day of judgment. It was Laestadius, therefore, who was responsible for the difficulty I had in taking pictures of the Lapps. He taught that it was a mortal sin to make a likeness of anything— except himself. His photograph today is found in many Lapp schools.

Although Laestadius deprived them of divining drums, the Lapps still have a most original way of finding lost articles. I discovered it when I saw Tuolja carefully place in his treasure box a black feather.

"What use is that feather?" I asked him.

"Of great use," he declared. "I can never lose a reindeer as long as I have this."

"Won't any feather do?" I asked.

"Oh, no," he replied quickly. "Only a raven's

feather, and then only a special one. A raven has only one finding feather, which is used to locate food."

I could not help thinking, as he spoke, how very closely he, with his superstitions and fascinating folk tales, resembled a Malay.

"How can you tell which feather to use?" I asked with great interest. His explanation was thorough.

"You must first catch a raven alive and take him to the bank of a running stream," he said. "There you pluck out his feathers, one by one, throw them into the water and watch until one feather goes up against the stream. If the raven still is alive, release it. Capture the feather and sleep with it for nine days. Then let the feather go in a strong wind and say the words, 'Come and be my guide when I need you.' Then, provided the raven has survived being plucked alive, you will be able to recover the feather. And it will always lead you to anything that is lost."

"Suppose the feather is blown away by the strong wind," I suggested.

"That will show," Tuolja replied, simply, "that the raven is dead and you must try another feather!"

While Tuolja was revealing these little tricks of magic, he was busily engaged in doctoring a sore on his hand. Since he was in a communicative mood, I plied him with questions and learned, so far as I could make out, that there were no Lapp doctors. But Tuolja knew the cures for many ailments.

For toothache he would fill the hollow tooth with tinder and ignite it! To cure blood poisoning, he would say: "That which has come from the mortal body of man shall there be no room for here. I order it away by the power of Lord Christ! Peace and health be to this person!" In saying this, he would take care to look intently at the sick spot. To protect his eyes from evil he would wear spectacles.

He knew also this infallible remedy for swelling: take some old sailcloth, preferably inherited cloth, soak it in tar, set fire to it and, while it is burning cheerily, apply it to the swollen part. Finally, Tuolja told me that the best cure for a stomach ache is to lie down and allow a dog to curl up and go to sleep on your stomach. Very soon the dog will get the stomach ache, having drawn it out of your body.

One day I remarked that the morning was lovely and sunny, and Tuolja answered cynically: "Early morning sunshine is like too much affection in a newly-married couple—it doesn't last long." The sunrise certainly did not last long. Within a short time it was pouring bucketfuls, and it rained steadily for the next fourteen hours. Although really fine, sunny weather is exceptional in Lapland, the question of weather does not bother the Lapps. They profess to control it.

"Suppose it rains—how shall I obtain a fine day?" I asked Tuolja. He answered: "All you have to do is to remember the names of nine bald-headed persons and then say, 'Nine bald-pates to heaven!' and throw a pinch of salt into the fire. Then there will be clear weather—if you believe it!"

Though I did not believe this there were many other things in the land of Santa Claus that I was forced to believe. That, for instance, you can be attacked by swarms of mosquitoes in spite of surrounding snow-fields—for these mosquitoes certainly bit me. That violets grow in large patches where a few weeks before deep snow has lain—for I picked such violets. That snow can be pink—Clyde Fisher and I saw plenty of beautiful rose-colored snow which, under the microscope, proved to be mixed with a minute, pink vegetable growth. I was forced to believe also that Lapps do all their burying in the winter—because I saw several "islands of the dead" from which, when cold weather comes, the Lapps exhume their dear departed and sledge them off to church for final rites. I learned, too, that these relatives of Santa Claus have songs which exalt profanity into an art, I know—because I have heard them.

And finally I came to believe in the very existence of hell, because just across the border of Lapland and Norway, I visited Hellemobottom—the bottom of Hell. There we found a tiny settlement of wooden shacks built by two Lapp fisher-families. Enormous bowlders would crash periodically down the almost vertical sides of the fjord and roll in among the houses.

"Why don't you move?" I asked one of the residents of Hellemobottom.

"Oh, I don't know!" He replied indifferently. Then he added: "You ought to see the flashes of lightning and the flying sparks when those rocks come down the mountain!"

The Hazards of Bathing

CHAPTER SEVEN

WHEN I left Lapland I returned south to Sweden for a bath. It was not because I did not bathe while in the land of Santa Claus, primitive as bathing conditions were, but because I wanted to satisfy my curiosity about a national institution which has made Sweden famous.

When I arrived in Stockholm, I discovered that there are many things besides the bathhouse for which that country is famous. There is, for instance, companionate marriage which the Swedish people now consider old stuff. And as for nudism they are far ahead of the rest of the world. They gave up being naked in private ages ago. Naked picnic parties, naked yacht parties, in fact anything naked is typically Swedish.

False modesty does not exist there as you will discover when you enter a Swedish bathhouse. Take your pet pekingese or your great dane, if you desire.

ADVENTURE!

Pay 50 cents, pass through a turnstile and be re-lieved of your valuables without fear. There are no thieves in Sweden.

You will be handed a small piece of canvas, about six inches square and too stiff to use as a towel. What on earth is it for? Be patient, and hang on to it like grim death, because you will need it in a moment. A girl will escort you to a kind of sentry box, or rabbit hutch, minus a door. You will enter the box, and while the girl stands on guard you take off every stitch of clothing. With a sweet smile she says in Swedish: "This way please."

She opens a small door and an amazing sight meets your startled glance. You find yourself in a miniature stadium with seats ranged tier upon tier, from floor to ceiling. When your eyes become accustomed to the terrific heat, you will notice men of all ages, sizes and shapes, sitting on little pieces of canvas and looking like boiled lobsters—the nearer the ceiling, the more they are boiled. Taking your seat on the grandstand's lower row, you gradually work your way to the top, where the purpose of the little square of canvas immediately reveals itself. Sit on it or burn!

After being thoroughly stewed you are escorted by still another girl to the scrubbing blocks. With-out any warning you are seized by two husky maidens, who place you upon a marble slab and proceed to scour you violently with a scrubbing brush. Finally a cold plunge awaits you, after which you are presented with a pair of enormous slippers and conducted down a long passageway to a weighing machine. I lost two pounds.

Upon returning to your sentry box, the girl whom you first met smilingly gives you all your clothes neatly pressed. Having watched you dress, she drops a curtsey, accepts your generous tip, and conducts you to the exit. There, to your delight, you find your dog, prancing around and wagging his tail. He has undergone exactly the same experience you have.

Bathing in a hotel is even more eventful. I shall never forget the first time I registered at Stockholm's famous "Grand Hotel." Having failed to secure a room with a bath, I called the room clerk at 7:30 a.m. and said:

"I should like to have a bath, please."

"You will have to wait till 8:30, sir."

"What's the idea of that?" I demanded.

"The girl doesn't arrive till then, sir," answered the clerk. So I waited.

Upon entering the bathroom at 8:30, I was greeted by a smiling female and a tub of steaming water. But, try as I would, I could not get that woman to leave the bathroom. The only Swedish

ADVENTURE!

I had learned was *"Jag elskar dig,"* which means "I love you," and that was of no use in this situation. There was nothing to do but hand the girl my pajamas. I stepped into the bath and, noticing a broad canvas strap which stretched from one side of the tub to the other, I sat on it. The girl burst out laughing.

She then pointed to my neck, whereupon I discovered that when Swedish gentlemen take a bath, they lie down in the water with their heads on the strap—for a very good reason which I learned immediately. Seizing me suddenly by the ankle, the girl lifted me up and soaped me all over! I had never been soaped like that since mother did it in a basin! Then the girl scrubbed me violently with a stiff brush, rinsed and dried me with a large bath towel, and that was that.

A famous friend of mine, who never had been out of America before, did little but take baths all the time he was in Sweden!

Once, while in Lapland, I was at a chalet where the Queen of Holland was stopping. A lady-in-waiting had ordered a bath to be in readiness for Her Majesty. Unfortunately, tubs are not of uniform dimensions, and not a word had been said of the royal displacement. The bath was directly over the chalet dining-room, and suddenly, into the dining-room, from the ceiling, came a drip, drip, regular and ominous. Diners frowned and looked annoyed. One of them peremptorily summoned the head waiter.

"Where is this water coming from?" demanded the upset guest.

A waiter scurried out to investigate with the manager at his heels. Presently the pair returned, silent and awed.

"It is very difficult to explain," said the manager. "It is not the plumbing. It is . . . well, it should not be mentioned, but the Queen, she is having her bath . . . and the bathtub . . . it is so very small!"

There was an immediate commotion among the ladies at a near-by table, and one did the graceful thing. Snatching from the table an empty water bottle, she reverently collected the now slackening patter as a memento—the bathwater of royalty.

Taking a bath in England has none of the Scandinavian glamour. The average English house is like an ice box even in midsummer and of all rooms in the house the bathroom usually is the coldest. Since every one will want a bath when you do, it is best to make arrangements in advance. Most English bathrooms are fitted with a geyser, and if you are very lucky there may be a supply of hot water "laid on." There is also an enormous piece of bath soap, usually disinfectant, a brush with a very long handle for scrubbing one's back, and a strange looking object, about the size and shape of a large cucumber, called a loofah, for scratching your front. This actually is the core of a tropical fruit. As soon as you turn on the hot water, the room becomes filled with dense steam. When you finish you find that English bath towels, called huckabacks, feel like the coarsest of emery paper.

It's a long way from London to Damascus where I had a delightful bath in the principal hotel, but even the second holiest city of Islam has its bathing troubles. I was one of a party of four. We had just returned from a dusty drive and all of us rushed immediately to our respective bathrooms, where we luxuriated in real Oriental baths. Each of us occupied a room on separate floors one above the other.

A Vassar girl had the topmost bath. I had the one under hers. Underneath me was a Texas Judge, and below him was my Brooklyn landlady, a Mrs. Grabbit, who, as she confided to me, had saved up all her life to make a Mediterranean cruise in order to go to Venice and have a ride on a "gondolier." Everything was all right until the Vassar girl finished her bath and pulled the plug. Immediately my bath filled with her bathwater, plus a dozen Spud cigarette butts. I leaped out of my tub and pulled the plug.

A muffled roar of anger told me that Texas had received my bathwater, plus the cigarette ends. As the Judge usually ate grapes when he took a bath, I can just imagine Mrs. Grabbit's feelings, when she suddenly was deluged with the remains of all three baths. I never shall forget the mournful wails that emanated from her bathroom when the deluge hit her.

For real bathing excitement you cannot beat Singapore. The first time I stayed at Raffles Hotel, I asked for a room with bath, but when I entered my bathroom, a small anteroom with a concrete floor, I could not find the bath. In a corner was a large earthenware jar about four feet high. Perched upon a little shelf was a small tin cup. A friend of mine in the next room evidently was in the same fix, except that he had managed to get into the jar and was now shouting for some one to get him out.

It was only instinct that told me what the proper procedure was. I stood beside the jar, dipped out water with the little cup and poured it over my head. This method of bathing is universal and wise in Malaya, because to lie in a cold bath may produce a chill, followed by death in the morning and burial in the afternoon. Things happen quickly in Malaya.

While I was gingerly pouring the water over my head I noticed two large frogs and five smaller ones hop out from behind the jar and deliberately take a bath with me. When I went out of the bathroom the frogs retired behind the jar. Every time I had a bath my seven frog friends joined me.

Light on the Dark Continent

CHAPTER EIGHT

AFRICA, the Dark Continent, with man-eating lions, fever, steaming jungles, gorillas, the dreaded tsetse fly, sleeping sickness, snakes that spit poison, and many other perils at which to shudder—that is the common conception of Africa. It was mine, too, to some extent, when I went there with the Massee Expedition of the Chicago Geographical Society and the Milwaukee Museum to photograph animals and climb the Mountains of the Moon. Scientists and veteran hunters did their best to disillusion me about the dangers. Yet it was not until I saw a motor car full of flappers and their escorts in evening clothes driving home through the lion country at 40 miles an hour, that I was convinced.

The dangers are not so bad as they sound. In fact you are safer in Kenya, Tanganyika, Uganda or the Congo than in most American cities. At least you don't run the risk of being held up or of becoming an innocent target for gangsters' machine gun bullets. If you go big game hunting the only danger you face is having some reckless driver crash into your car as you stalk a noble specimen of the King of the Beasts.

Take the advice of one whose knees shook as he contemplated meeting a lion without benefit of cage bars, and go to Central Africa. You'll get a new kind of thrill.

The first thing to do, is to secure a passport and a ticket to England. Although there are occasional boats that go direct, the sea voyage is very long and you miss all the fun of the trip through the Mediterranean. Let me caution you at the start not to make the mistake of the average amateur traveler who spends lots of money on an African outfit. Just pack your suitcase as if you were going to Chicago or any other modern place, because you will find that as you progress on your journey, you will be able to buy the clothing most suitable for your travels. Above all don't take any guns with you, not even if you propose to go big game hunting, for you will find that guns and ammunition cause more trouble and embarrassment with officials than anything else. You can buy all the guns you want in Africa and thus save heavy duties and all kinds of grief.

IF YOU WANT TO MAKE A LION "WILD," SHOOT AT HIM. IF
YOU KILL HIM, IT'S O.K., BUT IF YOU HURT HIM, HE WILL
PROBABLY KILL YOU.

THIS RHINOCEROS IS JUST AS FEROCIOUS AS THE ANT-HILL
—IF YOU LEAVE HIM ALONE.

ADVENTURE!

As soon as you arrive in London, get your ticket to Mombasa, first class, if you possibly can afford it. It will cost about five hundred dollars and a day's time for that ticket, because the powers that be are in no hurry to serve you. If by any chance you contemplate entering the Belgian Congo, be prepared to show the Belgian Consul two documents—one, certifying that you are in excellent health; two, that you are a person of unimpeachable moral character and that you have not had a relapse for the past five years! With those, your passport will quickly be visaed to the land of the "terrible" Ituri forest where there are excellent hotels and good roads to enable you to see the gorillas and pygmies at minimum discomfort.

Incidentally if you happen in at the hotel in Likasi, near Elizabethville, almost in the very center of the Dark Continent, you can get as fine a meal as you would in Paris. Here is what a friend of mine had there last Christmas Eve:

Aperitif
American Cocktail
Hors d'oeuvre riche
Creme a la Reine
Filet de sole spirate au citron
Asperges d'Argenteuil
Sauce Remoulade
Dindonneau farci a la broche

ADVENTURE!

Pommes-chips—Petits pois
Cochon de Lait
Sauce pommes
Pommes rissolees
Haricots verts
Glaces
Peches a la Melba
Gateaux de Noel
Friandises—patisseries—dessert noix
amandes—raisins secs
Cafe, fruits, fromages
Cigares et Cognac

Cigars, wines and liqueurs were free, the allowance for each guest was one bottle of white wine, one of red and one of champagne. The cost was 175 (Belgian) francs a head.

If you are not a good sailor you can save a week at sea by riding across Europe on the railroad and catching your boat at Marseilles or Genoa. But then you would miss Gibraltar. Gibraltar is an amazing place. It is not just an isolated rock or an island, but the most southerly part of Spain and is connected to the Spanish mainland by a narrow strip of land called the Neutral Ground. Gibraltar was captured from Spain by England in 1704. Many attempts were made against it, the last taking place in 1782 when English gunners bombarded French and Spanish besiegers with redhot cannon balls.

ADVENTURE!

Since then it has become the most famous fortress in the British Empire. As the story goes, England has no desire for a large population in Gibraltar, therefore it is illegal to be born there. Gibraltar is the home of the only ape found in Europe, the famous Barbary ape. Because of its short tail controversies have raged about the Barbary ape as to whether or not it is an ape. One group says apes have no tails, another contends they have. Anyhow it is a special kind of monkey that is easily trained.

You can see the coast of Africa from Gibraltar. If you want to, you can swim across. It has been done, but we can't stop to do it now because we pass into the Mediterranean and on to Marseilles. By this time you are almost sure to have made friends with many interesting people on the ship. There are all kinds, from big game hunters to typists returning to their jobs in Africa after a holiday at home. I remember meeting a policeman who was returning to Zanzibar. I asked him how he liked it and he said: "Oh, there are worse places, but very few. It's so windy there that when you land on the beach, the wind blows you right into the bar of the Africa Hotel where they serve whisky with lizards in it."

If you happen to be traveling through the Mediterranean toward the end of June, you may see one of the most remarkable sights in the world—a migration of painted ladies. I don't mean the human variety. I mean butterflies. They start from North Africa and travel northward often reaching Iceland. These beautiful insects nearly always buck the wind and have no difficulty in flying across the Mediterranean.

If you drop into the cathedral at Marseilles you will see the arm and hand of Gaby Deslys, that famous French actress and originator of the Gaby Glide, who used to dance with Harry Pilcer. Gaby Deslys left a great deal of money to the church and they have placed a wax copy of her beautiful arm on the altar of the chapel. And if your boat calls at Genoa you'll take in the dungeon where the most famous explorer of history wrote his travels —Marco Polo. While at the wonderful little island of Malta, famous for lace and cats, you will see people dressed in black clothes, the women wearing a peculiar cloak called a "faldetta" which is known as the cloak of shame. Although their troubles happened many centuries ago, the Maltese people still wear this strange mourning for the suffering they underwent at the hands of the early crusaders.

Then comes your first real thrill—setting foot on the soil of Africa at Port Said, the entrance to the Suez Canal. If you wish to, you may take the train to Cairo, visit the Pyramids and the bazaars, and meet your steamer at Suez. Thus you will "do" Egypt on the way to Central Africa. On the way home you can see the Suez Canal, constructed by De Lesseps, the man who failed to build the big ditch at Panama.

After leaving Suez, your boat enters the Red Sea and travels down the coast of Arabia. The Sinai Peninsula is on your left, but you cannot see Mount Sinai. And what is this Red Sea the Israelites crossed? Well, as a rule, it is blue, though at certain seasons of the year, when it is absolutely calm, enormous areas of the sea are a distinct brick red due to a microscopic organism floating in the water. This organism is neither a plant nor an animal, but a cross between the two.

Halfway down the Red Sea on the African coast is the Port of Sudan with a marvelous golf course on which there is not a single blade of grass. Its little red flags flutter gaily in sandstorms while vultures hover overhead waiting for some hole-in-one player to drop dead from excitement so that they can peck his eyes out. Then at Aden at the very end of the Red Sea on the Arabian peninsula you must be sure to see the "mermaids." There are several stuffed ones in the hotel, and the natives catch live ones occasionally, their proper name being dugong. Because it did not rain in Aden for several years,

Solomon had enormous water tanks built which are still in use.

As your ship passes Cape Guardafui you are near your journey's end, but it is advisable not to get shipwrecked here because some time ago the inhabitants ate the lighthouse-keeper. If you cross the Equator on a Castle liner you will not see Neptune. That old man of the sea has given up visiting the ships of that company ever since a woman was found drowned at the bottom of Neptune's tank after her husband had played the rôle of Neptune.

At last you arrive at Kilindini, the port of Mombasa. Look at the people—all colors under the sun, from African negroes wearing what look like Mother Hubbards, to proud Arabs (for heaven's sake *never* pronounce it *A*-rab) and groups of Indians faultlessly dressed in white duck with gold buttons. Here and there, carrying a long spear and a large leather shield, is a Fuzzy-Wuzzy from the Sudan, famous for giving England so much trouble in the days of Lord Kitchener, who finally subdued them. Their proper name is Hadendoa, and they come from the Red Sea province. They look like Gollywogs, and were given the nickname of Fuzzy-Wuzzy by Kipling, because their hair, about eight inches long, stands straight up on end not only from the top but all over.

ADVENTURE!

At the railway station a smart-looking train with two locomotives waits to pull you from the coast to the great plateau of East Africa. You will find that it is very hot after being so long at sea, but your spirits will rise when the station master says to you: "I have just had a hundred bottles of iced beer put on the train, sir." Almost as soon as you leave Mombasa the train begins puffling and blowing as it climbs higher and higher up the side of Africa. Stops at wayside stations bring out the wildest looking vendors from whom you buy all kinds of delicious fruit—soursops, mangoes, bananas and papaias. Soursops are about the size of cantaloupe, green and out of shape. Their name tells you how they taste. Papaias—sometimes called pawpaws—look like small green melons and are pink inside. They cure indigestion, the fruit being extremely rich in a kind of vegetable pepsin.

I used to bless the papaia when I lived in the tropics, not because I suffered from indigestion but because I used to suffer from tough meat! Native butchers used to kill an animal in the morning and sell it for beefsteak before it had stopped quivering. So I used to buy about two pounds of *moving* beefsteak, take it home and put it inside a papaia for about three hours. When I took it out it was beautifully tender and *predigested*. But that is not all that is remarkable about this fruit. You don't get any fruit upon a papaia tree unless you have both male and female trees, and for some unaccountable reason you often have a lot of male trees and no females. But that need never worry you, because as soon as the trees find out that they have no sweethearts one of the males turns into a female and everything is all right! Yes, the papaia tree can change its sex at will.

Soon the train passes through Tsavo, a nice, little town where thirty years ago a group of man-eating lions stopped construction of the railway by carrying away workers during the night. Not only would the lions enter the tents for men but they would take sacks of sugar out of the storehouse. The story of the man-eaters of Tsavo, however, need not raise any fear in your mind of being hauled out of your bed to make a meal for a lion. There was a good and valid reason for the lions of Tsavo to become man-eaters.

The coming of the railway with its noise and its many workers drove away the zebras and other animals upon which lions are accustomed to feed. Since the lions are by nature lazy, they refused to chase the zebras for miles and turned to the next best food —man.

They made their depredations nightly until the

railway was completed. When the country quieted down, the zebras returned and the lions went back to their usual diet.

If you keep your eyes open you will probably see a lion or two and some zebras from your window. The sight of the latter should reassure you that Mr. Leo still has plenty of zebra steaks and that there is little chance that he will go back to man meat.

But you soon will get bored looking at the animals. When you go to bed you will shiver under a blanket. If you get up early in the morning you will see what appears to be an inverted saucer floating in the sky. It is the summit of the highest mountain in Africa, Kilimanjaro, about eighty miles from the railroad. It rises out of the plain 20,000 feet and its top is smooth and covered with eternal snow. Some people believe that King Solomon is buried there. When I first went to Africa, I had intended climbing Kilimanjaro but I gave up the idea when I met an old man coming down with a walking stick!

As the train goes on, you will notice that the whole country looks like the prairies of America before the farmer plows them up. There are miles and miles of grass and small extinct volcanoes. Kilimanjaro itself is an old volcano.

At about half past two the train will arrive at

ADVENTURE!

Nairobi, capital of Kenya Colony, an up-to-date city with traffic cops. One of the first things I saw when I arrived there was a girl coming down the street in a fur coat. A little later, while I was standing on the steps of the Stanley Hotel watching the gorgeous African sunset, a man came up to me and said:

"You had better get inside out of the cold unless you want to catch pneumonia!"

Then I remembered that I had read a book on Africa by Mr. and Mrs. Martin Johnson who told how they got *double* pneumonia! So I went inside the hotel with the man who had warned me. He was Cherry Kearton, one of the most famous of all animal photographers and an old friend of the late President Roosevelt and Selous. We got warm around the bar where a group of men was standing in front of a log fire, swapping stories.

"So this is Africa," I said to myself. "Girl in fur coat . . . pneumonia . . . newsboys . . . log fires . . . and not a sign of a palm tree. Where is that terrible jungle they talk about in the movies?"

Of Nairobi's 13,000 population, 3,600 are whites. The town's streets are wide and well-paved and there are excellent stores of all kinds, especially outfitting shops for big game hunters. Nairobi is the Mecca for hunters.

ADVENTURE!

The language of the natives is Swahili and it doesn't take long to pick up a few words. Here are a few easy ones: *Missouri* means good, *toto* is a baby, and a *kuku* is a chicken. The word for fish is *samaki,* which please remember, for that is the nickname of Captain Salmon, the most famous elephant hunter in Central Africa, about whom you shall hear later.

Every other man you see is a regular Trader Horn, but there is one type, unfortunately very common here, called a Nairobi "stiff." He is the silly Englishman who says, "heah, theah, every-weah, doncherknow."

If you visit Nairobi market on Friday you will see an amazing variety of beautiful fruit, vegetables and flowers, all of which grow on the Equator. By this time you will be convinced that Africa is no longer the Dark Continent. The only really danger-ous parts of Africa are the deserts, and even there the danger is due to the fanaticism of the Moham-medan tribes who strongly object to Christians. Why, my nineteen-year-old son hitch-hiked his way from Lands End, England, to Nairobi, all by him-self. And he traveled to the very heart of Africa with a knapsack weighing sixty pounds, including a phonograph and twenty records.

Joy Riding Through the Zoo

CHAPTER NINE

I WANT you to imagine that you are actually sitting beside me in a motor car, and that we are driving along an African road from Nairobi to Tanganyika. You and I are in the back seat, and in the front, driving, is Pat Ayre, a famous lion hunter, who took the Duke and Duchess of York on their *safari* in Kenya.

By Jove, it's hot! Twelve o'clock, noon, the sun is directly overhead and there are no shadows. The road is bumpy and dusty. For the last hour we have been passing through richly cultivated country planted with coffee. Now the country is getting wilder. Gorgeous flowers grow alongside the road, blue in color and looking like forget-me-nots. This "wildest Africa" begins to resemble a park, with its large open spaces covered with grass and here and there beautiful flat-topped trees. Still there are no palms. What do they mean when they talk of jungles? They do not exist. It is too dry here.

Hello! Here is a nice little wayside store. I'm thirsty, so let's stop and get a cool drink. Here comes the storekeeper—a white man.

"Any chance for a drink?"

"Sure. Iced beer, if you want it."

"How do you keep it so cool?"

"Very easily. We're so high up here that it often freezes at night."

Well! That's astonishing enough, and a fine way to keep beer in condition.

Now we're off again. It is five o'clock in the afternoon, and we have arrived suddenly at the very edge of the Great Rift Valley. What a view! How big is it? As big as the Grand Canyon? Bigger, much bigger. Why, this valley could easily be seen from the moon if you were up there, for the Rift Valley is the biggest in the world.

It is beginning to get dark now, although my watch shows only 5:30. The sun sets at 6 o'clock all year round when you are on the Equator. Say, let's put on our sweaters. It's cold. That's more comfortable, you must admit. . . . There's our camp, those nice, green tents all pitched in a row, and over there is the cook's fire. Now we are motoring over the grass toward the tents.

"Blow your horn, Pat. Here come the servants carrying lanterns."

The stars are out already, yet it is only 6 o'clock. Those over there are the Southern Cross. Gosh, I'm shivering. Where is that overcoat of mine? That's a lot better. Now how about some supper in a hurry? Blessings on the man who invented baked beans.

Pat says we get up at 4:30 to-morrow morning. How about going to bed?

Better lace up the tent on the inside, because there are plenty of hyenas here. They may be cowardly animals, but they have a way of dragging a man out of bed. Well, good-night and pleasant dreams.

"What's the time? Man alive, it's 4:30 already. Well, here's the boy with hot tea. How did you sleep? Frozen stiff?"

It is pitch dark. The Southern Cross has gone. Over there is the Dipper. Let's have our breakfast out here under the trees, oatmeal, bacon and eggs and coffee. What a meal for the "wild" jungle! Can you hear those screech owls, and the birds waking up? Listen to those doves cooing.

The stars are fading now. Our men are taking down the tents and loading up the trucks. Here comes the cook with our bottles filled with boiling water. It's time to start. We're off again with the sun. We set our watches at 6, because for camp purposes sunrise is 6 o'clock.

How lovely everything looks, with the sun lighting up the tops of the extinct volcanoes all around us! Pat says the last time he camped here, he saw an airplane parked beside the road. Well, well! Wild Africa certainly is going modern.

Now we are driving along a trail as rough as the ones that used to cross the American prairies in the old days—just a couple of wheel ruts through open country. Look! There's a secretary bird, just catching a snake and killing it by jumping on it.

What's up now!

The car stops with a jerk, and Pat leaps out to examine the road.

"Lion tracks," he announces.

On again. See that jackal. He looks just like an American coyote as he calmly watches the car go by only five yards away. There are at least six varieties of jackal in Africa. Look over there, quick! At least a hundred zebras—and four giraffes! Those other animals are Grant gazelles, and here are some congonis.

Congoni is the African name for hartebeest. There are about nine varieties, all of which not only look stupid but really are. I'd just as soon shoot a domestic cow as a congoni!

ADVENTURE!

Those zebras are a bit shy or they would not be galloping off in such a cloud of dust. Aren't the tommies marvelous little animals? These gazelles are only about two feet high. You can't mistake them because they have a broad black band on each flank like the waterline of a ship. The Grant gazelles are larger and much harder to see, since they have no waterline like the tommies. Isn't this just like a ride through all the zoos in the world?

Look at the ostriches now, eight of them. Those black ones are the cocks and the gray are the hens. One of their eggs scrambled is enough for six men. By the way, did you know that all the other animals, including lions, apparently are afraid of the ostrich? If you watch animals drinking at a water hole, you will see how they declare a truce, mixing up in the most friendly fashion. But when an ostrich wants water, all the animals make way for this biggest bird in the world and allow him to drink by himself.

It is 7:15 a.m. and still quite chilly. Now what? There's a skeleton by the roadside with three black crows perched upon it. Death! Well, things happen quickly in Africa. An animal can be alive and well one minute and within an hour find himself a pile of clean-picked bones. See those tiny specks up there? Those are vultures and marabou storks waiting for some more animals to die.

Hello! We are quite close to a little extinct volcano. Pat says there usually are some lions in its crater. Let's see.

"What, no lions this morning?"

"No, but plenty of ticks."

Let's leave the ticks alone. Look down there on the plain where those great herds of game are feeding peacefully. The giraffes have seen us and are galloping away—just as you would see them in a slow-motion picture. Yet they probably are doing forty miles an hour.

Those beautiful cranes standing in that pool of water apparently are not a bit afraid of the car. Say, I have an idea. Let's see how fast some of these animals *can* run. Let's time that Grant gazelle.

"Blow the horn, Pat, and then watch your speedometer."

"What's that? Thirty miles an hour! Why he's only strolling beside us!"

"Step on it, Pat."

"Well, I'll be blessed! There goes the gazelle dashing across our bows and into the brush at forty."

Let's peel off our sweaters. It is 9:45 and getting hot again. That's the worst of Africa. Last night the temperature went down to fifty and now it is getting to be a hundred. Let's stop over there for lunch, at one of Roosevelt's old camping places.

It is as hot as the hinges of hades now. The heat waves are shimmering and the animals are no longer feeding on the plains. Instead, they are standing in groups under the flat-topped thorn trees. Thank heaven we humans have sun helmets.

Now it is 3:30 and beginning to cool off. Look! That enormous herd of animals over there resembling American "buffalo" are gnus. They are the scraggiest, thinnest "buffalo" you'll ever see, with long white beards and horns much longer than a bison's. The females have horns, too. Now the entire herd is galloping madly toward us. Don't be frightened. They are just curious. Here they are, close to our car, stampeding, darting from side to side, bucking like bronchos—and smothering us in black dust. Pat has stopped the car until the whole herd thunders past. They actually whisk the radiator with their tails which are used locally for fly swatters.

"Let's get out of this. Step on it, Pat."

Now we are past the dust. It is 4 o'clock, and here are Mrs. Wart Hog with five nice, little, striped wart hog babies trotting gaily behind her with their tails stuck straight up into the air. Our speedometer reads thirty, but they are simply trotting.

ADVENTURE!

"Blow the horn, Pat, and let's make them move."

These African wart hogs are a wild boar of small size but enormous tusks. Those in the upper jaw sometimes are a foot long, but those in the lower are only about five inches. If you chase a wart hog, he can dig a hole very quickly and—slide down into it backwards.

Still we motor on, crossing ravines and splashing through streams. It certainly makes my hair stand on end to see the chances we are taking. This is not the way I expected to risk my life.

"Hush! Don't speak!"

The car has stopped suddenly. My heart is thumping like a sledge hammer. Straight ahead of us are nine pairs of yellow ears sticking up over the long grass. Lions! Nine of them, all in a row, and they're watching us. We can feel that peculiar sensation of being watched.

Now the car has started again, and Pat is driving slowly through the long grass toward the ears that stick up only a hundred yards away. Seventy yards . . . fifty . . . closer and closer. Still the ears do not move. What excitement! We are speaking in whispers. Hand me my camera, quick! One big-maned lion is slowly standing up. He does not like the look of us and slinks away.

"Say! he's gone and left the lioness behind!"

ADVENTURE!

The King of Beasts, eh! Deserting his wife.

Now the car has stopped, and we are surrounded by more than a dozen lions, some crouching, others sitting on their haunches and gazing curiously at us like big cats. Not a sound. Not even a growl.

Pat has started the car and is deliberately driving through the ring of lions. He bumps a couple with the front wheels, and they slink off like a pack of frightened dogs.

It is getting dark now, and Pat suggests making camp near water. But look at the water—just a small pool of green slime. Well, up go the tents and out come the water stills. It won't be long before we are drinking that green slime and thanking Providence for it.

Our ride is over. The incidents I have described are not imaginary but are taken from my diary which actually was written as I sat in the back seat of a car while driving through Kenya to Tanganyika.

Bored by Lions

CHAPTER TEN

WHILE in Tanganyika my job was to get motion pictures for the museum of wildest Africa's best-looking animals. To give you some idea of how dangerous this business was and of the hair-raising escapes we had, I am going to put down just what took place every day. If I emerge from this narrative a hero, it is only because the facts speak for themselves.

.   .   .   .

After we had a bath, a shave and a hearty breakfast, Pat Ayre would come over to my tent.

"What's on the program, today, Wells?"

"Well, let's see. We need some zebras. How about getting some?"

"Right you are. Let's go."

After checking the equipment and seeing that our water bottles were filled we got into the car and dashed off through the "jungle" at 40 miles an hour until we came to some zebras. On this morning we happened to encounter about 800 of them. They were quietly grazing and we drove up close to look them over.

"How many do you want?" Pat asked.

"I have an order for six," I replied. "The museum wants a male, a female and four little ones."

"Well, there are a lot of family groups here, take your choice."

It did not take long to find a family which answered the specifications and take all the pictures and notes needed.

"Let's call it a day," I said to Pat and we drove back to camp to kill a few hours until it grew cooler. It's too hot to hunt or photograph animals around noon.

The next morning Pat came again to get a line on the day's work.

"How about a few giraffes today?" I asked.

"Righto!"

Off we dashed again and before long came to a herd of giraffes. They looked like telegraph poles on the horizon and were just as active. We stopped the car within a hundred yards of them and got out. When I got close to them—at least 10 yards—I noticed their eyes were closed. The giraffes were asleep!

Here was a pretty state of affairs. How was I to get motion pictures of animals that didn't move? I clapped my hands and they opened their eyes. They looked me over from head to foot and still didn't move. I walked up to the tallest brute—he was about 16 feet high—and took a panorama of him. He seemed to like being photographed. Finally I shooed him away and got a very funny picture of all of them running with their long forelegs while their short hind legs went at a gallop.

"This is getting boring, Pat," I said, as I went back to the car. "Let's go back to camp and have a cocktail."

Our cook made excellent martinis and so we whiled away the day.

The third morning Pat came again.

"Let's do something exciting today, Pat," I said. "How about a few lions?"

And so again we dashed off into the "jungle" at 40 miles an hour.

We were in luck. We found 18 of them lying in the shade of a tree. Actually there were 19 because one of them was up in the tree. I guess that fellow had personality and objected to being just one of the herd. Those under the tree were all in a heap as if they had been emptied out of a sack. As the car drew close several of them raised their heads gave us a bored look and turned over and went to sleep again.

"Are they any good?" I asked Pat.

"What's the matter with them?"

"I don't see any manes on them."

"All lions don't *have* manes," replied Pat. *"Must you have maned lions?"*

"The museum wants them maned," I said.

"Oh, well," said Pat with a shrug, "We needn't bother about these then."

So we left them, still lying down, and drove along until we came to two magnificent specimens—a sleeping lioness with her mate standing beside her. The male had a huge black mane and looked just like those outside the New York Public Library— and he probably roared just as often.

"How about these?" asked Pat.

"Great," I said. "Drive up closer." At 15 yards I could see a big scratch on the male's shoulder.

"He won't do, Pat," I said. "The museum wants a good clean specimen. That fellow is all scratched up."

"The big ones always get scratched, Wells," replied Pat. "Let's go on. Wait a minute; why not have a look at him on the other side."

We drove around the lions who watched us with

a morning-after look (lions gorge themselves at night and sleep or loll about during the day).

The big fellow was all right on the other side and I took all the pictures I wanted. Once in a while they would look up at the camera and yawn but most of the time their eyes seemed to say "when are you going to get out of here and leave us alone?"

And so once more we drove back to camp for a cocktail.

.   .   .   .

Of course I do not want to mislead you, or to suggest for a minute that wild animals are not dangerous, because they are. You need only to visit the cemetery in Nairobi and look at the tombstones. They tell all about it. This man—mauled by a lion. Another chap—attacked by a leopard. Another— torn to pieces by a gorilla or sat on by an elephant. But the point is this: Animals are dangerous only *when they are wild,* and they *never are wild* until some one makes them wild. The easiest way to make an animal wild is to shoot at it. If you kill a lion, he won't hurt you. But if you hurt him he will do his best to kill you.

While I was in Tanganyika, a woman arrived to do some big game hunting. She never had done any before. Very few big game hunters have, until they arrive in Africa.

ADVENTURE!

This woman decided she would like to start by shooting a rhinoceros, "because they are so easy to hit." She did not know that ordinary lead bullets have no effect upon a rhino and that you must use special metal jacket cartridges. She happened to meet a rhinocéros while driving on the road and she shot it.

It took no notice of her and she shot it again. She shot it seven times before it looked up—then it tore her to pieces!

The next day the Nairobi football team was motoring over the same road. In the front car was the captain of the team and his wife. As they drew near to the scene of the previous day's disaster, they saw a rhino running toward them. It was not until the beast was nearly upon them that the man sensed the danger. He told his wife to get out, but before he could get from behind the wheel the rhino was upon the car. The woman saw the beast turn the machine over and kill her husband. When the other players drove up they shot the rhino and found seven lead bullets in its side. It was wild and had been waiting to avenge itself on another car.

Another big game hunter decided to hunt a buffalo on horseback. The buffalo tossed the horse, its horn entered the horse's chest, came out of its back, pierced the saddle and killed the rider.

ADVENTURE!

Then there was the famous lion hunter who decided he would shoot elephants for a change. He and his son set out in the morning to chase an elephant. That same afternoon, the son brought his father home in a sack.

What usually happens, however, in so-called big game hunting is this:

A man suddenly gets tired of shooting ducks, or perhaps of *trying* to shoot a moose, and decides to graduate by going to Africa to shoot lions. Arriving in Africa, he immediately hires a "white hunter" (white to distinguish him from natives) who takes him out in an automobile. This white hunter is not only a chauffeur but is a crack shot as well.

The amateur duck-hunter sits next to the professional lion-hunter, with an arsenal of guns beside him on the running board. Among the rifles is sure to be an elephant gun, which in all probability never has been used because the hunter is timid about firing it. Usually the white hunter carries a double-barreled rifle, standing ready in a frame. Soon this pair meets a lion. The car stops, and the lion pays not the slightest attention to them. None of the animals, except monkeys and hyenas, who seem to have special intelligence, recognize any danger in an automobile.

The amateur gets all a-twitter.

"Shall I shoot it?" he asks excitedly.

"Sure," says the professional. "That's what we're here for!"

The amateur selects his rifle, usually a gun fitted with telescopic sights, so that he can get all the thrill of being very near the lion when the animal is fifty or even a hundred yards away. He takes aim. He is trembling with excitement. His rifle wobbles.

While his attention is fixed upon the lion, the professional lifts his own rifle which is fitted with a hair trigger and aims carefully at the same animal. He waits with his finger ready.

Bang!

It is the rifle of the amateur. But the concussion of his gun sets off the professional's and down goes the lion. Before the amateur has recovered from the shock of shooting *at* his first lion, the professional is calmly smoking a cigarette, his rifle back in its rack on the car.

White hunters have told me that seventy-five per cent of so-called big game hunters never hit anything but the sky.

Once while sitting in the lobby of the Stanley in Nairobi I heard an amateur big game hunter who had just arrived from the field, tell of his first encounter with a lion.

"Did the lion charge?" some one asked.

"No," frankly replied the amateur. "But you can bet that by the time I get home it certainly will."

Hugged by the King of Beasts

CHAPTER ELEVEN

IF you are ever faced by a charging lion don't shoot him through the heart. It won't do any good. In fact it will increase his speed in your direction. Many a hunter has heaved a sigh of relief in such a situation, as he sees his bullet has struck in the vicinity of that vital organ, only to find that the lion is upon him and clawing him to death. In fact lions shot clear through the heart have been known to inflict mortal wounds or severe lacerations before the bullet has taken effect.

Such is the story of Colonel C. L. R. Gray of Arusha, and through the courtesy of "The Field," I reproduce it here:

Last September three lions killed one of my bulls. I went out with "G." and found the kill two-and-a-half miles away, partly eaten. We heard the lions moving about in the bushes, but could not get a glimpse of them. I arranged to have a *machan* (platform) built in the biggest tree in the vicinity, and had the kill dragged to within ten yards of the tree and put in a fairly open patch of ground; the country generally was covered with bushes five feet high or grass three feet high.

At sunset I was up in the tree with my guns, a 12-bore loaded with ball and buck shot and a .333 Jeffery with an electric torch attached. I bowled over the first lion about ten minutes after sunset, but he got up and crashed away. The second lion got a good bullet and died less than a hundred yards away.

About 2 a.m. I heard lion No. 3 prowling under my tree, investigating thoroughly; eventually he came to feed with an eye kept on me, vanishing at the slightest movement. After one or two attempts I at last got a snap at him; he answered once to the shot, then galloped right away, and I was doubtful if I had put in a good bullet.

At dawn my men arrived, and taking my magazine rifle I went to look up the dead lion, intending to change to the 12-bore when I searched for the other two. The men were in a blue funk, and I could not get them up in line with myself, so I went on. They followed fifteen yards or so behind me. Suddenly there was a grunt and No. 3 launched himself from about thirty or forty yards away. I saw nothing but his head. Crouching low on the ground with his eyes concentrated on me, his mouth shut, he rushed forward at terrific speed, dividing the bushes as he came. He was traveling smoothly, his head extraordinarily steady. He appeared to be nothing but head, which got bigger and bigger. I realized that I had no time to put in two shots. I decided to brain him at five yards.

As I fired he swerved to the left and I missed his brain. Except for a scarcely perceptible pause, the shot had absolutely no effect. I might have been using a pea-shooter. I saw the skin on his shoulder quiver where the bullet went in. He came straight on without a sound; he did not spring at me, but kept low until his head was about three feet away, when it suddenly rose out of the ground. I cannot remember what happened next. When my brain again functioned I was still standing up in front of the lion, whose head was about three inches above mine and two feet away. My arms were stretched out, hands about one foot apart, my fingers were dangling down close to the lion's nose; my rifle was gone. I felt extraordinarily limp, as though I had been sandbagged. The lion's mouth was partly open.

With incredible quickness, and snarling as he did it, he went snap, snap, snap, biting me in the left wrist and hand, finishing up on the right hand. He then dropped to the ground keeping hold of my right hand, turned sharp round and pulled me into the bushes. I walked along his left side, incapable of resistance. After a few yards he let go, cantered slowly away and left me standing in the bushes. I walked out, lay down to recover, and the men, coming up, told me the lion had got up on his hind legs and put his arms round my neck. I refused to believe this statement, as I felt positive I had not been touched by the lion before he bit me. I had never even seen his arms.

A most unpleasant trek home, where "G." helped me to syringe the wounds and then took me to hospital. I was quite at a loss to understand why the lion had not knocked me over. Why was I feeling so slack, and what had I done with the rifle? "G." came in next day and said he had been out with some officers of the K.A.R. (King's African Rifles), and found two dead maned lions, one a huge one. The third, gushing with blood, they had tracked into impenetrable bush, where they were certain he was dead. He had also found my rifle with the woodwork at the back near the magazine bitten right out and a piece of tooth broken off and buried deep alongside the barrel.

Three days afterwards my clothes were brought back by the *dhobi* (laundry), and I noticed the coat and shirt were both ripped down the back of both shoulders. Two scratches, skin deep, were then found at the back of one of my arms. So the lion had touched me with his paws after all. One could then reconstruct what happened.

The lion must have smacked his heavy paws at the back of my shoulders, proposing to hold me for a hundredth part of a second while he fastened his teeth in my throat, then forcing my head back would have toppled me over with a broken neck, instead of which his teeth, crashing on my rifle, which had been thrust out across his mouth, must have given him the shock of his life. He must have jerked his head back, thus ripping my coat, then wrenched the rifle from my grasp and sent it flying. His wounds by this time were affecting him, and with an aching jaw he was afraid to bite hard, simply snapping at my hands.

Some days afterwards his carcass was found, but unfortunately some native had found him first and removed his head and skin, so I have never recovered his skull with the broken tooth.

ADVENTURE!

Stories similar to the one told by Colonel Gray led Dr. George W. Crile, an eminent surgeon of Cleveland, Ohio, and an expert big game hunter, to make a study of the physiology and psychology of lions.

Dr. Crile began his experiments on antelope. He found that with a shot in its heart and sometimes when that organ had been completely severed from the arteries, an antelope could continue to run up to 100 yards. This, he decided, was due to the nervous energy which the animal had stored up before it was killed.

He then made careful tests on lions. He discovered that the king of beasts can run up to 50 yards and in one case up to 100 yards with a bullet through its heart and still have strength left to kill a man.

The next thing to do was to find a spot in the creature's anatomy which, when struck, would paralyze it. After dissecting a few of the beasts he found what he was looking for. It was situated between the spine and shoulder. He came to the conclusion that a well-placed shoulder shot just beneath the spine would stop a lion instantly.

He had to wait until he and his party tracked down a lioness and two cubs before he could test his theory. Suddenly, without warning, the doctor found himself within 18 feet of the lioness which was crouched and ready to spring to protect her young ones. Here was a case in which the lioness had to be dropped in her tracks or Dr. Crile would have to give up his experiments. To make the situation worse other members in the party were scattered around in a way to put them in danger from his bullets.

Catching the animal's eye Dr. Crile slowly began to kneel and aim for one of his expectedly paralyzing shots. He made dead certain before he pulled the trigger.

Nothing happened. The lioness still crouched. Just as the doctor was ready to shoot again, one of his party signaled him to withhold his fire. The animal was stone dead. Dr. Crile's shot had paralyzed her.

The technique now used by many as a result of the paralyzing shot is for the hunter to stare the lion in the eye. As the beast is not accustomed to have its prey stand ground, he usually swerves in his attack. This exposes his shoulder for the nerve shot. Even if the shot misses the nerve center, it is likely to hit a mortal spot. In either case the hunter is safe as the animal cannot turn and will plunge ahead in a straight line until it finally falls dead.

Dr. Crile also brought the American cowboy's "creasing" shot to Africa. This shot, by which the cowboy sends a bullet through the fleshy part of an animal's back or mane without touching the spine, passes so close to the spinal column that the shock causes temporary paralysis. The animal falls, apparently dead, but later gets up with only a slight flesh wound. This shot is sometimes used to get live specimens of big game.

According to Cherry Kearton, the big game photographer, a lion often has a thorn-like spike on the tip of his tail which he uses to lash himself into a fury when he gets ready to attack. Whether or not that is the purpose of the spur I do not know, but one of the lions we killed for the museum had a spike on his tail such as Kearton described.

A lion cannot chase its prey over long distances. That is because its muscles are made for springing. A hundred yard dash would leave him winded and spent. While his bones are small, his muscles are huge. His brain, too, is small and lies in a flat head. Thus to shoot a lion through the brain when he is facing you is a real test of marksmanship.

The question of brains is interesting. The larger and more compact an animal's brain is the quicker it dies from a brain shot. A snake has only a small part of its brain in its head, the remainder is distributed throughout the length of the spine. That is why a boa constrictor will continue to crush after its head is cut off.

Aside from being short-winded and having a small brain, a lion has a tender skin. In that respect it differs from a giraffe who has an epidermis at least an inch thick. He may, from this, appear to be a pretty tough fellow, but I can recommend giraffe steaks as being tender and succulent. A lion must be skinned at most 10 minutes after death. Sun is fatal to his hide. Immediately after shooting, skinners put up a temporary shelter, under which measurements and photographs are made for museum taxidermists. The hide is then salted and dried in the shade while the animal's skeleton is put up in a tree. Hide and skeleton are numbered carefully so that none of the taxidermists at home will put the head of a lion on an elephant.

Although lions are poor runners they are good ventriloquists. They are the only creatures I know of that make any real use of that trick. If their prey is near by they can roar as if they were a mile away. In this way they deceive the animal they are stalking until they are within comfortable striking distance. If after springing, they fail to get their victim they never give chase. They look around for another one.

The king of beasts does his hunting at night and

sleeps in the early morning hours. Later in the day he can be seen trailing behind herds of animals which, at night, are his prey. The latter, strange as it may seem, show no fear. W. D. Hubbard, a deep student of big game, in an article in "The Sphere" finds this indifference difficult to explain but advances some interesting questions. He says:

Hunters not infrequently have seen lions walking among herds of antelope or zebra without causing a panic. Every such happening can be explained by the obvious fact that the lion was fully fed. But how did the antelope know that? When their dreaded enemy suddenly appeared among them, walking unconcernedly in daylight, how did they know that at this particular time the lion was inoffensive? Did they see, as human observers saw, that the stomach of the lion was heavy with food? Or was there some other indication which even professional hunters did not see or understand, but which was evident to the antelope?

The African buffalo has acquired a reputation for aggressiveness which is surpassed by few other big-game animals. Particularly is the buffalo feared when wounded, for then it resorts to tricks which have brought death or mauling to many hunters. A mortally wounded, or even badly hurt buffalo—and this is true of elephants also—will turn out from the herd with which it has been running and travel by itself. Once alone it will run a varying distance, depending upon the severity of its hurt. Eventually it will turn, and, circling, either come back close to its outward tracks or stand hidden to one side of its spoor. Hunters tracking carefully with their eyes on the ground follow the blood-bespattered trail. They round an anthill, cross a patch of long grass, and—whang!—the buffalo charges upon them from an unexpected direction, and at very close quarters. Only an exceptionally experienced hunter or a very fast shot can extricate himself from such a predicament.

Most of the lions I saw in Africa looked fat and flabby. They had sway backs and their stomachs flopped from side to side as they walked. How different they looked from those lovely, greyhound-like animals reared in California. In Hollywood, lions must preserve their graceful figures just as the movie stars.

Not long ago I saw an African picture made in Hollywood. Suddenly there appeared on the screen one zebra. Now I doubt if anybody ever saw just one zebra anywhere in Africa. One time I myself saw a herd 30 miles long and several miles wide. A little later out pranced a marvelous, stream-lined lion. From the look of amazement that came over Leo's face I suspect that this was the first zebra he had ever seen. Probably he thought that Mr. Zebra was a sport model, California jackass. When the lion started to chase this strange looking object, the zebra turned around and knocked the lion down! It was really pitiful. It made me think of Sim who I hope will never be like the lion movie actor.

ADVENTURE!

Sim is the pet of the Milwaukee Museum. He is now a full-grown lion. He was found after a prairie fire had laid waste miles of country in Tanganyika. When the blaze had spent itself, a cry was heard near the camp and the men found a lion cub about the size of a kitten. It was badly singed and famished. Fortunately we had in camp with us a goat and her kid. The three became fast friends but Mrs. Goat did not have enough food to satisfy the extra mouth and so Sim's diet of goat's milk was supplemented with malted milk. Sim—short for Simba, the Swahili word for lion—grew fatter and fatter on this sophisticated diet. He never showed any desire to go back to find his parents and romped about the camp like a dog. He used to go out in the car with the museum collectors and look at the animals. He seemed fascinated with it all.

Finally the time came to return to America. The expedition was returning via Paris and having no desire to put Sim in the way of temptation, it was decided to send him directly home. Into a large box went Mr. Sim and off he was packed to the captain of a steamer sailing from Africa straight to New York. A letter was sent with the box explaining that its occupant was a friendly soul and that it was safe to let him out of his box after the ship sailed.

The captain did as suggested and the two became

such fast friends that they slept together, the captain in the lower bunk and Sim in the upper.

Sim arrived safely in New York and took a pullman to Milwaukee where he moved into the taxidermy department of the museum because he had known the taxidermists in Africa. There he would sit by the hour watching the men stuff his relatives.

It was some time later before I reached Milwaukee and when I called upon Sim, he rolled me over and over and playfully took my head in his mouth. Eventually he got too big for the museum and was placed in the zoo where today he is as playful as ever despite the fact that he weighs over 300 pounds.

Rhinos Have Moustaches

CHAPTER TWELVE

A CAMPFIRE on the plains of East Africa with the Southern Cross gleaming in the heavens and with the evening breeze blowing cold, is always a gathering place for story tellers. Outside the circle of firelight, crickets drone and from afar comes the hunting roar of lions.

On this occasion we had been talking of tight situations and how coolness of mind and a little straight thinking will often save a man's life.

"Yes," said Martin Johnson, the American big-game photographer, "I had an example of that only a few days ago. The Boy Scouts, who are staying with us to learn something of the habits of big game, and I, decided to get flashlight pictures of lions. We placed a big iron cage in the truck from which we could watch what went on in safety and drove out a few miles. We put the cameras on tripods and rigged up the flashlight apparatus so that the lions would set off the flashes and take their own pictures.

"We waited for several hours and when nothing happened I suggested that we go back to bed. The boys, however, insisted on staying and I left them in the cage. No sooner had I gone than there appeared a whole troupe of lions—eight of them. One of them set off the automatic flash and then the fun began. They knocked down the cameras and tried to eat the steel cases. Then they discovered the boys in the truck. One clawed the tires and another jumped on the driver's seat. As he placed his paws on the steering wheel he touched the siren button. As it sounded the whole gang of them jumped to the ground.

"Discovering that the noise was harmless they leaped back on the truck and tried to get at the boys.

"Now these youngsters, instead of getting panicky, held a meeting about what should be done. One suggested firing their rifles to drive the beasts away. But they all agreed that wouldn't do because I might hear it and thinking they needed help, would rush right into that gang of lions. They decided that the cage would withstand the lion attack and remained there until morning when the lions wandered away.

AN UNUSUAL PHOTOGRAPH OF MALAYAN JUNGLE DWARFS OR
"SEMANG" WHO MEASURE ABOUT FOUR FEET THREE INCHES
IN HEIGHT. THESE DWARFS WERE NOT AWARE THAT THEIR
PHOTOGRAPH WAS BEING TAKEN.

AN AFRICAN SPEAKEASY—THEY LIKE THEIR DRINKS COLD.
THEY HAVE BURIED A BARREL OF BEER AND SIT AROUND IT
SUCKING UP LIQUID REFRESHMENT THROUGH LONG STRAWS.

"That's what I call cool thinking. Many a grown-up would have lost his nerve and fired under those conditions. The funny part about the incident and one that gave us many a laugh, was the picture of the boys in the cage surrounded by lions. It was the zoo reversed."

Johnson also told us that living among Africa's big game often got boresome and they would set themselves to thinking about what could be done for excitement. On one occasion they decided to go fishing for lions. They attached a strong rope to their car and used a dead zebra for bait. Off they started dragging the bait slowly through the jungle past some likely looking bushes in which lions usually rest during the heat of the day. They had not gone far when two sprang at the pair. Of course they did not try to land the lions because, if there is one thing that a lion objects to, it is being landed. After playing them for a while they cut the rope and left the beasts firmly attached to the bait.

Of all the African fish stories I've ever heard, the funniest is about several Englishmen in Zanzibar who did some serious drinking and then went out trolling. In a little while one of them got a bite. Instead of the line going down it started to travel up to the sky. All of them saw what happened but each was afraid to mention it for fear that he was seeing a new manifestation of pink elephants. When the fishermen finally came out of their mental fog, they found that an eagle had snapped at the bait, grabbed the line and headed skyward with it!

Pat Ayre is reminded of a story.

"Johnson's yarn about the boys," he said, "reminds me of Banks. He is the Government elephant hunter of Uganda and one of the original hunters of the Lado Enclave. Banks is a man who has spent his life getting out of tight situations. On one occasion he was camped at Victoria Nyanza with his pet fox-terrier, a fearless little fellow to whom Banks was very much attached. After smoking a pipe over the campfire he brewed himself a cup of tea, placed it alongside his bed in the event that he should be thirsty during the night, and turned in. Suddenly he was awakened by the frantic barking of the dog from his place beneath the cot. The flap of the tent had been left open and Banks saw a large leopard standing near the bed watching the terrier. Leopards, you know, are very fond of pet dogs.

"Banks never slept without a loaded rifle and shotgun within easy reach. He realized, however, that these weapons would do him no good. The leopard was only an arm's length away and the movements necessary to reach for the rifle, push up the safety catch and aim would give his visitor ample opportunity to spring upon him. Glancing around, Banks saw the cup of tea. He grabbed it and flung it in the face of the leopard which bolted into the bush. Banks slept undisturbed for the remainder of the night."

An interesting fact about leopards is that they have been known to wander up to the snow line in some of Africa's mountains. On one occasion, while I was well up around 12,000 feet, I came upon a shelter under a ledge where a leopard evidently had reared a litter of cubs. How she lived when the small antelopes she prefers for food rarely venture into the rarefied atmosphere is something I can't explain.

Dr. S. A. Barrett, director of the Milwaukee Public Museum, then told a story of how fickle rhinoceroses are. He had been driving through the "jungle" several days before and had seen a rhino standing behind a bush. The doctor stopped his car to see what the big fellow would do.

It evidently had never seen a car before and became very curious. It walked up to the machine, and, probably thinking that it looked like some huge animal, decided to scare it. He backed away for several yards and then rushed at the auto. Dr. Barrett is a man with plenty of nerve. He kept the motor running and waited calmly for the charging animal.

When the rhino reached the car and found that his "enemy" held its ground and did not run away, he stopped in amazement. Getting up his nerve again he smelt the radiator, burned his nose and ran for dear life. Never before had it met an animal with such a hot nose.

One of the men, however, objected to calling a rhino fickle and said that he had seen one of them attack a tractor and smash it to bits.

The rhinoceros incidentally has no horn. The protuberance on his upper lip may look like a horn and feel like one but in reality it is a waxed mustache. It is not attached to the skull.

That so-called horn is greatly prized by the Chinese who grind it up and turn it into love pills. So big is the demand for these love pills in China that the animal is rapidly being exterminated. In fact there are only about 130 of the great white rhinoceroses left in Africa. White men spurn the use of the horn as an aphrodisiac, but instead they make wheels out of the rhino's hide.

Hippopotamuses, on the other hand, have little to offer the world of commerce and they are generally left to live their sluggish lives in peace. One of their favorite habitats is the lovely lake of Elementeita which is full of soda and has no fish. When the hippo wants a drink he has to crawl out of the lake and explore the land for a pool of fresh water.

Africa's wild pigs, for some reason, appear to me to be a small edition of a rhino, to judge from a story told me by a shopkeeper in Nairobi whose wife had lost her umbrella.

It seems that the handle of the umbrella had been made from the curved tusk of a wild boar and that the lady would not be happy until she had another just like it. So the husband went out to shoot an umbrella handle!

He soon met a fine old tusker, raised his rifle and pulled the trigger. Nothing happened, except that the pig became annoyed at the gun and started to chase the hunter. The man flung away his weapon and ran for his life with the pig at his heels. After doing a record quarter mile, the pig became disgusted, gave up the chase and turned back! To this day, declared the hunter, his wife won't believe he even intended to get her another umbrella handle.

"Talking of tight situations, charging rhinos and wild pigs," said one of the taxidermists, "in my opinion the most dangerous animals in all of Africa are those damn jiggers. At least you know when a lion is coming at you but you can't see these pests."

"You're right," agreed Pat. "They came in here from South America. They usually burrow under the nails of your toes or fingers and it's the devil's own job to get them out. The best thing to do is to let a native extract them with a blunt pin. If you let them stay in they breed enormously. They are so bad in Uganda that natives have been known to hang themselves in despair."

I think the jigger is even worse than the much dreaded tsetse fly, the sleeping sickness carrier. Dr. Crile, inventor of the nerve shot for lions, told me that sleeping sickness can be accounted for in areas believed safe from it by the fact that wild animals during migrations carry the infection.

The tsetse fly looks like a gray horse fly but is a bit smaller. Its wings fold one over the other instead of being side by side as on the flies we know. The insect has two proboscides, one of which juts out in front, while the other, which may be infected with the germs of sleeping sickness, sticks out at right angles. His bite hurts until he puts his proboscis into you. After that, while he is swelling up to the size of a large pea, his activities cause no pain. Later, however, you may sleep if you want to or not. I was bitten dozens of times by tsetse flies but all the time I was in Africa I suffered from insomnia.

Aside from tsetse flies there are plenty of insects in East Africa. Fights among scorpions, tarantulas and cockroaches constitute regular sports in Kenya. I have seen a cockroach rush in between a scorpion's pincers and bite off the latter's head.

During the war a camp of 3,000 soldiers was completely captured and the soldiers put to flight by big black scorpions six inches long. The camp had been pitched on very dry land where rain had not fallen for months. A downpour came in the middle of the night and immediately the ground belched swarms of scorpions—at least six to a man. There was nothing to do but abandon camp for the night and lay siege to the scorpions in the morning.

Later in the evening the conversation swung around to treachery in animals. Most of those present agreed that this quality is rare in beasts.

"The most treacherous creature I know of," said Pat, "is the honey bird. He is a little smaller than the English sparrow and as you know, he is supposed to lead men and animals to nests of honey. More often he is in league with a lion or tiger and the bird will tempt you to follow him into an ambush.

"Once while hunting in Uganda we were attracted by the antics of a honey bird. We followed it and in half an hour it began to show signs of excitement. Sure enough right near the scene of its frenzied fluttering we found honey. The bird watched us until we finished and when we started away it began again to entice us. Thinking that he might lead us to more honey we followed and stopped in time to see a lion about 40 yards away which we shot.

"Later my boys told me that the bird led us to the lion because we did not share the honey with him."

The story that has thrilled me more than any of the many others I heard while in Africa was that of Captain Salmon's encounter with a wounded elephant. Captain Salmon, or to use his nickname, Samaki, the Swahili word for fish as I have already said, was about to go on leave. Like most Government officials he had very little money saved. He decided to make extra money by shooting a few elephants for their tusks. As Government elephant hunter he had shot over 2,000 and had little trouble obtaining permission to shoot 20 for his own use. He already had 18 and on the day about which this story centers he set out with his gunbearer to get the last two. It was not long before he was following the trail of two fine tuskers.

Having shot elephant Number One, Samaki walked on past the dead animal and shot elephant Number Two. While he was examining the second, he was amazed to see the first elephant get up and rush past him into the bush. Knowing that the animal must be badly wounded, Samaki and the gunbearer pursued and followed the wounded elephant's spoor until five o'clock in the afternoon. Even then they could not see the elephant. From the marks on the ground they were sure it was concealed in the elephant grass close to the main roadway. This grass often grows over 12 feet high. It looks like thin bamboo but it is practically solid and very stiff, like cane.

Finally they found a sort of tunnel in the grass and into the tunnel went Samaki. He was making his way cautiously when without any warning the huge animal charged down upon him. He fired one barrel of his rifle but the elephant rushed on and seized him in its trunk. In some way Samaki managed to hold on to the rifle. He placed the muzzle against the animal's right eye and fired. The bullet went right through but even that terrible wound failed to stop the elephant. It tore the rifle out of Samaki's hand, wrapped its trunk around the man's neck and shoulders and swept him round and round, clearing a large open space in the tough grass.

While the elephant was using Samaki as a scythe, the gunbearer, an extremely brave man, picked up the rifle and tried to hand it to his master. Like a flash the elephant, which somehow had lost one of his tusks, dropped Samaki on the ground between its legs, struck the bearer with its trunk and dashed out his brains.

Then holding Salmon wedged between its legs, the beast began to play with the dead body of the native, turning it over and over, occasionally stopping to feel the dead man with its trunk. For a moment Samaki felt the animal relax its hold on him and he started to crawl. He was only about three feet away when he realized that the brute was playing with him as a cat with a mouse, for the elephant grasped him by the ankle and gently dragged him back between its legs.

The next time the beast relaxed his hold, Samaki, who was covered with blood, had the presence of mind to wriggle under the elephant's stomach. As soon as the animal missed him, it began to prod the ground with its one tusk. Fortunately for its victim, that lone tusk was on the elephant's blind side and it kept missing its prey, sometimes only by inches. Meanwhile Samaki managed to keep under the beast's stomach.

At last, being unable to get hold of its victim again, the brute raised its hind foot and kicked Samaki in the back. The blow paralyzed him and left him unconscious. Thinking that his prey was dead, the elephant ran his trunk over Samaki and shambled into the grass.

ADVENTURE!

How long he lay there he does not know. I saw him as I started for the Mountains of the Moon. He had just come out of the hospital and was still bandaged.

"What's the next thing on your program?" I asked. He laughed.

"Why, I'm arranging to take the Prince of Wales elephant hunting," Captain Salmon replied.

He not only took the Prince out but he brought him back as well.

Elephants Never Forget

CHAPTER THIRTEEN

EVER since I had my first ride on an elephant in a circus, these enormous animals have always fascinated me. I have known them in Asia and in Africa and although the Asian variety is superior in intelligence, the African elephant still remains a noble creature. In fact, when I came back from Africa I missed elephants so much that I began collecting them. They are all around me right now, on the table, the mantle and on the bookcase, as I write. I guess I am not the only person who is fond of elephants. I have given away about 10,000 of my little friends similar to the one on the title page of this book. And once while speaking on the radio in Chicago I promised to give an elephant to any one who asked for it. I received 7,000 requests.

To tell where an elephant comes from, look at his toe-nails first. If he has five nails in front and four behind, he comes from Asia. If he has four in front and three behind he comes from Africa. Or, if you don't like counting toe-nails, look at his trunk. If he has one tip on the end of it, he comes from Asia. If he has two tips, he is from Africa. If, however, you cannot see the end of his trunk just look at the trunk itself. If it is just an ordinary smooth-looking trunk, he is an Asiatic, whereas, if his trunk appears to be made in several segments, he is African. Another way of identifying an elephant is by his ears. The ears of an Asiatic elephant are about two feet long and rather ragged. The African's ears are about the size of a piano. I know a woman in New York who had an African elephant's ear made into a dining table at which she seats ten people.

If you go elephant hunting, you will find that in both Africa and Asia, elephants object strongly to being shot at. In fact, they are likely to charge you. If, in your excitement, you forget whether you are hunting in Asia or in Africa, you can find out by the way in which the elephant comes for you. If he curls his trunk up into a ball, holds it in front of his head and charges silently, you are in Asia. If he screams and rushes at you with his trunk straight out—then you are in Africa. You can make absolutely certain by looking at his back. Asiatic elephants are hump-backed; African elephants are sway-backed—like the lions.

ADVENTURE!

In one respect, however, Asiatic and African elephants are alike. Both have stomachs so enormous that it is almost impossible to keep them filled. Therefore elephants are always feeding. Some authorities say that they eat twenty-four hours a day. However that may be, they eat heartily. I once saw an elephant knock down a tree and devour it, trunk and all, as if it were celery.

White elephants of Siam are not really white at all. They are pink and have large bluish spots showing through the pink skin. When you see a really white one in the circus, the chances are that he's been whitewashed. But pink, white or black, an elephant can walk almost as soon as he is born, invariably is a good swimmer, and usually has one offspring at a time though now and again there are twins.

Have you ever noticed what a short neck an elephant has? It is so short that when he eats you can hear his food tumble into his stomach with a splash. Of course you won't hear the splash when you give an elephant a peanut.

If you want to know the height of an elephant, it is not necessary to measure the animal. Take the circumference of his front footprint and multiply it by two. This will give you the height at the shoulder.

Though elephants have a convenient supply of teeth, they use only four at a time, two in the upper jaw and two in the lower. They do not renew their teeth as we do. Their molars are always moving forward. That is to say, the new teeth do not come up under the old ones. Instead, they appear behind the old and push them ahead in a groove, until eventually the old ones slide right out. An elephant's tooth often weighs twenty pounds.

An elephant's tusks grow about ten feet long and weigh more in Africa than in Asia. Many of the biggest Asiatic elephants have no tusks at all, except when they are babies. They are born with tiny milk tusks which soon drop out.

The record weight of one tusk is about 240 pounds. With ivory worth about five dollars a pound, you can easily see why elephants are hunted.

But you can't walk right out and shoot all the elephants you want in Africa. You must first get a visitor's hunting license which costs about $500 and then you must take out a separate elephant license. In Kenya a permit for one elephant is $250 and for two, $750. If you should shoot one whose tusks weigh less than 60 pounds, you must turn them over to the government and take out a new license, providing the permit you have calls for only one.

While African elephants are hunted for their

ivory tusks, those in Ceylon have been the principal source of supply for circuses since the days of the Romans. A Singhalese elephant is seldom shot hence there is always a great supply of them. Their footprints are to be found from the lowest valleys to the summits of the highest mountains.

A curious thing, and probably the saving grace, of elephants in Ceylon is the fact that not one per cent have tusks. Both sexes of the African variety possess these great teeth; the females of the Indian breed usually have very small ones while the Singhalese have only apologies for these ivory protuberances known as "tushes."

The idea that the tusks of an elephant are his weapons of offense is probably entirely incorrect. Tusks are used for digging and it is interesting to note that in countries where elephants have to do a lot of digging in order to obtain food, their tusks have developed correspondingly. In Ceylon, elephants can find an abundance of food without rooting and that probably explains the deterioration in the size of their tusks until they are now only rudimentary. When fighting elephants rely on their enormous weight, their strength and on their trunks.

And yet these big beasts rarely fight. Sir James Tennent, one of the greatest authorities on elephants, in commenting on their relations with each other, is of the opinion that: "the elephant lives on terms of amity with every quadruped of the forest, that he neither regards them as his foes, nor provokes their hostility by his acts; and that, with the exception of man, his greatest enemy is a fly!"

The ancients believed that elephants had no joints in their legs and even Shakespeare was uncertain about it:

> The elephant hath joints; but none for courtesy;
> His legs are for necessity, not flexure.

For many years it was thought that elephants could not lie down whereas the truth is that their legs are almost as flexible as man's. Elephants are able to lie down and get up with more ease than a horse. They are extremely agile and can ascend heights which man finds extremely arduous. Elephant tracks have been found on the very summit of Adam's Peak in Ceylon, 7,420 feet high, which pilgrims climb with great difficulty by means of steps hewn in the solid rock.

Provided there is room and solidity to sustain their great weight, elephants are so sure-footed that there are few places they cannot go. I have descended a river bank at an angle of forty-five degrees on the back of an elephant when the animal stretched his fore feet out in front and his hind legs behind and slid down on his stomach with the greatest ease.

In India, Ceylon and Malaya (probably in Africa as well) a herd of elephants is a family. One doubts the family theory of the African species because of the great number found in the herds of that country. On several occasions in Asia, complete herds have been captured and examination and study of each group showed that its members had the same family characteristics.

The herd is an exclusive circle and its members do not associate with those of other herds. If an elephant is accidentally separated from its family tribe and unable to find it again, it is just a lost soul, or rogue. Other herds bar it, although they may tolerate the outsider near by or even allow it to drink at the same watering place. But intimate association is strictly taboo. That is probably why rogues are bad-tempered.

Tame elephants which escape into the jungle also become rogues because of the elephant law barring the outsider from the herd. The tame rogues are most dangerous to man as they use every trick taught them by their former masters when free of their dominance. They take delight in pushing over houses and sometimes will wreck entire villages and deliberately destroy gardens.

I once saw a rogue untie some native boats and set them adrift. The same elephant then entered a rubber estate and proceeded to empty the china cups hanging on the trees to collect the rubber.

The leader of the herd is not necessarily chosen for size or strength but for courage and sagacity. And most of the herd leaders in Asia are females! Elephants are always devoted to the leader and will protect him or her from danger. When a leader has been wounded, other elephants have been seen to support him with their shoulders and help him escape.

When safe from further harm the injured one makes a surgical dressing of grass which he places in his wounds. These are changed from time to time until the hurt is healed.

Elephants, like camels, can store up water after drinking it and when necessary regurgitate it. An example of this, which lovers of elephants will read with disgust, is given by Gordon Cumming in a "Hunter's Life in South Africa." He says:

"Having fired thirty-five rounds with my two-grooved rifle, I opened upon him with my Dutch six-pounder, and when forty bullets had perforated his hide, he began, for the first time, to evince signs of a dilapidated constitution. Throughout the charge he repeatedly cooled his person with large quantities of water which he ejected from his trunk over his sides and back, and just as the pangs of death came over him, he stood trembling violently beside a thorn tree, and kept pouring water into his bloody mouth until he died!"

Personality in animals is especially noticeable in elephants. Some are brave while others are very timid. Elephants, as a rule, run away when wounded, but I know of one that pursued the man who had wounded it. It actually followed him into a village, trampled him to death in the bazaar before a crowd of terrified spectators and then succeeded in escaping into the jungle.

Elephants are inferior to most animals in sight, hearing and scent. I know of a man who was tracking an elephant through the jungle in Malaya and actually bumped into the animal's rear end. The elephant was as surprised as the man. I know of another man, in Africa, who made a bet that he would write his initials on the stern of the biggest bull elephant in a large herd. Taking a piece of chalk, he walked through the herd, selected the largest bull, chalked his initials on Jumbo's hind quarters and won his wager.

Does an elephant forget? I don't think he does. At least not the one I used while surveying in Malaya. This elephant took a violent dislike to a small dog that used to run in front of him and snap at his toes. One day while I was riding him back to camp, we passed the dog fast asleep under a tree. The elephant stopped, kicked a large piece of dirt in the dog's direction, but missed. We went on to the river bank for a bath. As I was mounting him to return, he stirred up the water in a pool and filled his trunk with mud and stones. The dog was still asleep when we got back and the elephant squirted the contents of his trunk on the poor pup who scurried off, yelping with fright.

Most people have heard about the man who was kind to an elephant in the jungle and how the same elephant, while performing in a circus many years later, saw the man who befriended him sitting in a twenty-five-cent seat. He immediately walked over to the man, lifted him tenderly from the cheap seat and set him down gently on a two-dollar cushion.

One thing about an elephant that has always interested me is that he never allows himself to suffer very long from indigestion. If an elephant eats something that disagrees with him, he simply puts his trunk down his throat and into his stomach, from which he sucks up the contents and squirts it out.

Despite all the stories we hear about their ability to remember, elephants are not as intelligent as dogs, although their brain is slightly larger than man's.

You can train an elephant to be almost human, yet no elephant has volunteered his services to man. You might be murdered right under the nose of your pet pachyderm and I doubt whether he would interfere. He'd probably run away.

The story that an elephant is afraid of a mouse may or may not be true. I know, however, from my own experience that elephants are afraid of caterpillars and millipedes. They also object to anything unusual in the jungle.

While surveying in Malaya, I used to mark out the way with wooden pegs, sometimes with posts. These posts were usually of hard heavy wood about four feet long and six inches square. We would hammer them into the ground until only a foot was above the surface. This would be painted white so that it could easily be seen. Time and time again elephants would deliberately pull up these posts and fling them fifty or sixty feet into the branches of trees. They would also object to my camping places and, while I was away, they would smash up my happy home, taking special delight in stamping on my pots and pans.

A question which all amateur big game hunters take delight in discussing is where elephants go to die when they grow old. I, too, thought it was a mystery until I discussed the matter with experts on elephants in Africa.

When an elephant feels age creeping upon him or when he is sick or badly wounded, he leaves the herd. Most animals are cruel to the weak. The first thing he seeks is water and because of his weakness makes his way to low lands, generally marshes to eliminate the need of climbing steep banks. Eventually he becomes bogged and being too weak to extricate himself, sinks into the mud and dies, often disappearing completely from sight. Several hunters have actually seen them in bogs and one was able to make an excellent picture of an elephant down to his belly in a quagmire. When I think of the fact that bones of ancient animals are found around water courses, the explanation strikes me as being an extremely logical one. It is generally conceded that elephants live to the age of about 60 years, although there is on record a most exceptional case of a tame elephant attaining the age of one hundred and forty.

While working in Kedah, a Malay State not in the Federation, I heard from natives that elephants go to die near a small village called Sok. Not long after I heard this story I happened to be in Sok and I asked an old headman if he could tell me of the place where elephants go to die. The man smiled.

WE REARED SIM ON GOAT'S MILK AT FIRST, BUT HE PERSONALLY
PREFERRED MALTED MILK, BECAUSE THERE WAS
AN UNLIMITED SUPPLY.

ONE YEAR LATER, PLAYFUL AS A KITTEN BUT RATHER HEAVY!

ADVENTURE!

"It's ridiculous," he said. "Sok is a regular health resort for elephants. They come when they are sick to drink the hot water which bubbles out of the ground. It is *obat* (medicine). Elephants who think they are going to die come here. They generally go away feeling better than ever."

Where I thought I was going to find an elephant cemetery, I found a fountain of youth.

If we are to believe an inscription on one of the Egyptian tombs, Ptolemy Evergetus was the first to capture and train African elephants for military use. There is evidence, too, that African elephants were employed by the Carthaginians in their wars.

Hannibal, also, knew the value of elephants and had a number of them with him when he invaded Italy by way of the Alps. It is on record that he halted his army for three days in those mountains while a road was made for the great beasts, but how he managed to feed his elephants on the march still remains a mystery. An elephant requires 500 pounds of green food a day.

Carthage had stables for 600 elephants, a number which certainly could not be fed in one town on the Mediterranean coast of Africa today. The Romans used African elephants in their gladiatorial games and reckoned them inferior to the Asiatic breed.

The writer is indebted to the weekly newspaper, *East Africa,* published in London, and to Dr. J. M. Bechet for the material on the domestication of elephants which follows:

After the fall of Carthage and Rome the domestication of the African elephant was abandoned, and the secret of it was lost until, by the enterprise of Leopold II, King of Belgium and founder of the Congo Free State, and the skill and devotion of Commandants Laplume and Magnette and their assistants, MM. Vermeesch and Henrotin, success was once more achieved.

Laplume began his attempt to domesticate the elephant in 1895 at Kira-Vungu, on the Wele, and by 1899 he had succeeded in taming twelve. After a lapse of five years he returned to the Congo to find only eight of his herd left, and these he removed to Api, which he rebuilt as an elephant training station.

Api is a pretty little place, built on a broad, red road running beside a slow river, with neat bungalows gay with flowers, round native huts, and an elephant *kraal,* two and a half acres in extent, surrounded by a strong palisade made of posts fifteen inches thick bound together by interlaced bushropes.

The secret of the taming of the African elephant, as rediscovered by Laplume and Magnette, is kindness. No one in the camp at Api is allowed to strike, tease, or in any way annoy an elephant. Unremitting kindness and silence are the rules enforced, for the animals are easily upset by noise. Even the click of a visitor's camera is enough to set the young captives screaming and pulling at their chains, and motor cars in their neighborhood are unthinkable.

The capture of the elephants presented many and great difficulties. Pits were tried at first, but proved useless; the *keddah* method, as practiced in Ceylon, failed owing to the impossibility of handling the mob of captives of all ages, and eventually they had to be released. Finally it was decided to cut out a cow and her calf from the herd, kill the mother and heel-rope the young one. With the aid of the Azandi tribe, a fearless race of hunters and warriors, this method proved successful, though care has to be exercised as to the age of the captive. It was found impossible to rear suckling calves, as nothing could replace the milk of the elephant, which is extremely rich in fats. Now only weaned calves are caught; they are strong little beasts and full of fight.

Even when caught much remains to be done and there are many difficulties to be surmounted. Although the elephant has a thick hide, it is easily cut by ropes and special soft but strong ones are used. Wounds of any sort, even superficial, especially in the limbs, often prove fatal in spite of antiseptic dressings. Some captives just lie down and die as if broken-hearted; others thrash themselves to death in their struggles when caught. For weeks after capture there is danger that the animals will refuse food, pine away, and die. The tame elephants may even attack the newly caught, and in nine cases out of ten the result is fatal. Then there are disease—worms, diarrhoea, prostration, fever, and, above all, sunstroke, for the African elephant is a forest animal which must have shade during the heat of the day. In spite of all these pitfalls, the tame herd at Api numbered twenty-five in 1921, of which fifteen were females, forty in 1925, and the number rose to about seventy in 1927.

ADVENTURE!

These elephants are trained to definite kinds of work:
(I) draught, i.e., pulling trucks mostly loaded with cotton, and ploughs; (II) carrying light pieces of wood in
the trunk; (III) shifting logs of timber; and (IV) up-
rooting trees, bush and stumps. When qualified, each elephant receives a diploma, as it were. Some, however,
never take to certain kinds of work, so that in the Api
list you will see that "Boma," a female, 7 ft. 1 in., is
fully qualified for all four kinds of work; "Faro," a
male, height 6 ft. 4 in., can do everything but carry logs;
while Moganga and Albert, little things of 5 ft. 8 in.,
can do only light work with small timber. This shows the
minute care with which the elephants are treated and the
attention paid to their idiosyncrasies. It must be added
that careful measurements are regularly made, so that
the rate of growth of each animal is known.

The day at Api begins at five o'clock in the morning
for elephants not working. They go to the feeding
grounds accompanied by their mahouts. They return at
6 p.m. and are given a ration of cassava and sweet
potatoes or a few bananas. Working beasts commence
at 4 a.m., or even at 1 a.m. or a little later if they have
far to go. In every case they knock off at 11 a.m. for
rest, a bath, and a noon meal. Sometimes they resume
work at 4 p.m., when the sun is getting low, and work
until sunset, when they have another feed and return to
the station.

Each has its own stable, but these are used only in
the rainy season. In dry weather and on moonlight nights
the animals sleep where they like in the *kraal* and may
feed on and off, instead of sleeping. Plenty of water for
drinking and bathing is absolutely essential to their

health. Unfortunately, they do not, if left to themselves, keep clean long, for they love to roll in dust or mud after their bath and get incredibly dirty. This rolling is forbidden at Api.

The trained elephants at Api are perfectly obedient to the word of command, are intelligent and docile, but they never forget an unjust reprimand or punishment. Several men have been intentionally killed at Api by tame elephants, but as there was always proof that it was the fault of the men, nothing was done to nor did an elephant kill any other person.

As to the financial side of the understaking, full details are lacking. Up to 1913 the ivory obtained in the hunts fully paid all the costs of the station. In 1925 the Api budget amounted to 443,000 francs, which, compared to the value of the elephants and other by-products of the station, was considered in no way excessive. According to Mrs. Grace Flandrau, who visited Api recently, when an Api elephant is sufficiently grown up—and this may take ten years—he is sold or rented to planters; and, quoting Commandant Magnette, she adds:

"The overhead costs to the man who buys him are very low. Elephants don't consume gasoline, and they find their own food in the bush. A pair of elephants can haul a four- or five-ton truck thirty kilometres a day, or plough three acres in a morning. They are particularly good at clearing land and hauling logs. The wear and tear is small if they are well treated, and they outlive many masters. In fact, they become stronger and stronger during the first hundred years, which is more than you can say of a Ford."

Apes I Have Met

CHAPTER FOURTEEN

THE gorilla, despite his size and strength, is not as dangerous as many fiction writers would have us believe. Gorillas don't carry off white girls to their arboreal homes. They have enough trouble with their own women. Such stories about this anthropoid (resembling man) ape arose probably because of the fact that he is the largest of the primates, a biological classification which includes man. Man is by nature a worshipper of brute strength—consider the popularity of heavy-weight boxers and wrestlers—and because of his interest in muscular idols is inclined to make fables and weave mysteries about the object of his worship, even though it be a gigantic ape.

The gorilla is by nature peaceful and like all other animals is not wild until some one makes him so either by shooting or otherwise annoying him. Man, too, under similar circumstances, is prone to imitate

the gorilla. In this respect, at least, they are alike.
I do not desire you to assume from this that I am
offering more evidence to prove that man descended
from the ape. I leave that controversy to zoölogists
and theologians. I want merely to tell you about a
few apes I have met.

Many persons confuse monkeys with apes. They
are absolutely different animals—in fact, there is
more difference between monkeys and apes than between apes and men. Apes have no tails and include
the gorilla, the orang-utan, the chimpanzee and the
gibbon. I have handled them all. In my opinion the
most intelligent is the orang-utan; the one that most
resembles man is the chimpanzee; the largest is the
gorilla and the most affectionate the gibbon. The
gibbon is the only one of the four great apes that
naturally and habitually walks erect. Of course I
do not include the one in "Tarzan." That's a special
breed which lives only in the imagination. Orang-
utans and gibbons live in Malaysia; gorillas and
chimpanzees live in Africa.

It would not be fair to the visitor in Africa nor
to the gorillas not to pay a visit to their home in
the vicinity of Lake Kivu between Lake Edward
and Lake Tanganyika. The lake itself is 5,000 feet
above sea level and the gorillas are 5,000 feet farther
up. The climate at that height is cold and therefore

gorillas wear thick fur coats. When full grown these big apes are generally six feet in height and weigh over 400 pounds. They have small ears, short, stumpy hands and feet very much like our own and even have a regular heel, a member which other apes do not possess. The gibbon, conversely, has such long fingers and toes that he can place his hand on one ear and scratch the other with the same hand.

Gorillas prefer dense bush. They spend most of their time on the ground making tunnels through the underbrush. They will climb trees to gather fruit and tender shoots, but they are conscious of their enormous weight and do not swing around carelessly as do the smaller apes. Gorillas are like Chautauqua artists—they sleep in a different bed every night. When bedtime comes the gorilla builds a substantial nest on the ground or in a tree in which the females and the young sleep. The male usually sleeps on the ground at the base of the tree to be ready to protect his family. Chimpanzees and orang-utans build nests like the gorilla but the gibbon never troubles to make a home for himself. His home is where he hangs his arm.

The gorilla is essentially a vegetarian and his favorite food is parsley and wild carrots. Physical culturists or wrestlers may try gorilla food and see if they obtain the strength of this big ape. So far as is known the only use he makes of his enormous muscular power is to break down branches to build his nest. None of the apes like the hot sun. In fact, they are so fond of the shade that they are extremely difficult to photograph.

The gorilla was first made famous by Paul du Chaillu, the Franco-American traveler and explorer who died in 1903. In fact, most of the scientific world regards him as the discoverer of gorillas and pygmies, and the American Geographical Society presented him with a large silver cup in recognition of this discovery. In all probability gorillas and pygmies were discovered long before du Chaillu was born. At least pygmies were known before Christ. Du Chaillu's accounts of the gorilla were indeed terrifying. He told of its tearing men to pieces; snatching away their rifles and destroying them; walking about with a large stick in its hand and in general behaving like a demon of the jungle.

His discovery probably inspired the motion picture "Ingagi," which was supposed to be the true story of a gorilla who carried off a woman. Unfortunately, the gorilla in the picture was a man— and the only real apes in the film were orang-utans —and they don't live in Africa at all!

The gorilla fable was exposed by that famous American explorer and scientist, the late Carl Akeley, who made a special study of these great apes. He hunted them, photographed them at close quarters and came to the conclusion that they were like all other animals when unmolested. Within the last few months Akeley's observations have been substantiated by Martin Johnson, who not only has secured some wonderful motion pictures of gorillas but captured three live ones and brought them back to America. Johnson admits that gorillas are probably the most terrifying of all African animals— especially the old males. They would often rush at him until they were within a few yards of his camera —evidently doing their very utmost to frighten him away. When Johnson held his ground and continued to crank his camera, the gorilla would suddenly stop his rush, turn around and run! Had Johnson lost his nerve and fired at the gorilla, there would either have been one less gorilla or no Martin Johnson. In either case, some one would have accused the animal of charging. It never pays, however, to generalize about animals. It may be that Akeley and Johnson had the good luck not to meet a gorilla with personality. There is no doubt at all that some animals are endowed with a very decided personality. That's why some lions like to climb trees, and some hippopotamuses object to people playing golf. Perhaps the best instance of personality in an animal was the famous elephant, Jumbo, whose eccentricities have been told in song and story.

When du Chaillu reported that gorillas would attack a hunter and actually seize his rifle, he was discredited, and for many years his stories in general were supposed to be exaggerations. But not so very long ago members of an expedition to the Cameroons in West Africa, reported that gorillas in that district were far more ferocious than the ones near Lake Kivu. They even discovered that the natives in the Cameroons hunted gorillas with home-made rifles having barrels made of gas pipe! A native would load the pipe with powder and shot, deliberately approach a gorilla and allow the animal to grasp the gun barrel. When the beast attempted to bite it, the native would pull the trigger and the gorilla's head would be blown off! Several of these old gun barrels, bent out of shape by gorillas, were found by the Cameroon expedition. Thus du Chaillu may not have been such a liar after all.

The three gorillas that Johnson brought back with him were a pair of large ones about the size of an eight-year-old boy, but already much stronger than a man, and a baby about the size of a two-year-old child. They were quite a handful for two men to manage. The large ones were kept in captivity but the baby made itself at home in Mrs. Johnson's apartment at the Hotel St. Moritz in New York. On several occasions they took the baby to see the old couple at the zoo. The little one would rush up to the female and hug her. Then father gorilla would embrace the baby. Often the female and the baby would walk off together and go inside a box where they would probably have a long talk. If we could have understood their conversation, I expect we would have heard the little ape tell the mother how Mrs. Johnson allowed it to use her lipstick and powder.

Many attempts have been made to understand gorilla language but without very much success. Their habit of drumming on their chests is thought to be a means of communication. They make a loud booming sound using both hands alternately. The movement is so rapid that their hands appear to be a blur.

In captivity gorillas do not seem to be nearly as happy as chimpanzees and rarely live as long. They are particularly subject to chest ailments even in the wild state and can often be heard coughing.

Just as the elephant is known for his long memory, the ape is famous for his imitative ability. In fact, we use the word "ape" in the same way as the word "imitate." I think one of the best instances of imitating was described by the great explorer, Stanley. He told of the case of some chimpanzees that stole a native drum from a village. The apes carried it to the very top of a tall tree where they beat it vigorously. This may have been the origin of the jazz orchestra.

Chimpanzees make wonderful pets until they become conscious of their great strength and then, although they are just as clever as before, they are apt to be dangerous if angered. A friend of mine had a chimpanzee for several years. It always lived with the family and had its meals at the same table. It was an unusually intelligent creature. One evening my friend happened to be called away unexpectedly and as there was no one at home, he locked the chimpanzee in an empty room. The animal did not seem to mind being locked in and remained very quiet. Curious to see what the animal was doing, my friend took a peep through the keyhole. The chimp was doing the same thing—looking at his master from the other side of the hole.

The best ape story I ever heard came from Missouri. The St. Louis Zoo is probably the finest in America and contains an excellent collection of anthropoid apes. Some time ago one of the keepers went into a cage of one of the largest chimpanzees to investigate a commotion. As he opened the door the chimpanzee slipped out and locked the keeper inside.

The situation was especially comical because it happened during the lunch hour when the ape house was absolutely deserted. Try as he would the keeper could not get out because his hands were too large to pass through the cage and unlock the door. As he struggled to free himself, Mr. Chimpanzee proceeded to explore the ape house.

He deftly opened a door leading to the basement where he found four workmen enjoying their lunch hour. Three were playing cards while the fourth was cooking some hamburgers on a stove. Into this quiet scene walked the chimp. The four men had no desire to entertain this uninvited hairy guest and they stampeded out of the basement yelling for the keeper. Imagine their amazement when they found him jumping up and down in the cage recently occupied by the chimpanzee. For a moment they thought it would be safer to leave him where he was but when he explained his presence there they unlocked the door. All five men then rushed to the basement where they found Mr. Chimpanzee standing before the stove turning over the hamburgers.

Collisions with Snakes

CHAPTER FIFTEEN

I ENCOUNTERED few snakes while in Africa but that was just a case of hard luck. I was anxious to get camera studies of them but evidently they were not in the mood to pose. Africa, of course, has many snakes, the best known being the mamba, the cobra, the puff adder and the python. But nowhere are there as many dangerous snakes as in India and Malaya.

Snakes kill about 20,000 persons in India every year. These fatalities may be compared to the number of deaths sustained in traffic accidents in the United States. They occur as a result of running over snakes, or to be more specific, stepping on them. The common cobra is sluggish and has a habit of sleeping where he cannot be seen. You step on him and like a flash he has sunk his fangs into your foot. At night he likes to stroll around gardens and will even enter houses. Naturally he cannot be seen in the darkness and as a result we have more collisions with snakes resulting often in death.

Little or nothing is done to eradicate cobras because many of India's 300,000,000 people regard that reptile as sacred. A legend has it that the original cobra was once chased by a large snake-eating bird. Just as he was about to be devoured, he called on God for help. The snake's faith in his Creator was immediately rewarded. According to the story, God caused a pair of spectacles to appear on the snake's extended hood. The bird was so frightened it flew away and never went near a cobra again.

While the common cobra enjoys living in houses where it is not uncommon for Indians to feed them milk "to appease their wrath," the king cobra, or the hamadryad, prefers to live in the jungle. He is the largest poisonous snake in the world and is regarded as the most dangerous because he has no fear of man. It probably is the only snake that will follow and deliberately attack a human being. It is notoriously bad-tempered and in zoos often attacks its keepers at feeding time. The hamadryad is a cannibal. It lives on other snakes but refrains from eating those that are poisonous.

An interesting story is told of the late President Roosevelt, who, besides being a real sportsman of the old school of big game hunters, was a great naturalist and interested in snakes. While studying snakes, he arranged a battle between a king cobra and the American king snake. Both were about the same size. The king snake, like the king cobra, is cannibalistic but not poisonous.

When the snakes were placed in the ring the usually bad-tempered king cobra immediately recognized the king snake as a dangerous enemy. He withdrew to a corner and watched every movement of his adversary. The king snake, too, sensed danger and moved cautiously. The American snake was the first to attack. Then a terrific battle ensued. They lashed at each other desperately and finally got tied up in a knot.

The struggle lasted only a few minutes. To the surprise of the onlookers, the cobra collapsed and died and the king snake calmly began to swallow his late adversary. He did not get far with his meal. His movements grew slower and finally ceased. An examination showed he was dead. In the mêlée he came in contact with the cobra's fangs and so the contest was declared a draw.

Snakes are not immune from their own venom or that of their own species. During a fight in which two cobras repeatedly bite each other, both invariably die. There is a case on record of a battle royal among seven Cape cobras during which all were bitten and all died.

Non-venomous snakes succumb rapidly to the bite of a cobra. Its poison attacks the nerve centers. The bite of a puff adder or viper is slower in effect causing internal hemorrhage. Puff adders, incidentally, have been known to commit suicide. One of them was brought fresh from the *veld* to the snake park of the Port Elizabeth Museum in South Africa. It was a wild, fierce creature and to calm it was placed in a glass bottle with a rubber top. When it was released a day or so later it turned furiously on its own body, drove both fangs deep into the tissues and was dead within a half hour.

The constrictor type of snake makes up for the lack of venomous fangs by a long body endowed with powerful crushing muscles. Practically all of them are harmless to man and even the biggest of them will run away at his approach. In Africa the biggest snake is the rock python. The largest in the Malay Peninsula is the reticulated python while the largest in the world is probably the anaconda of South America. There are many wild stories about the length of snakes but it seems very doubtful whether any have been found much over 30 feet. Snakes, like fish, vary in size with each story.

One of the most exciting adventures I ever had

with a python occurred in the Malay jungle. I was surveying a straight line for the railroad and was standing behind my transit directing the Malays ahead of me as they cut down vines and small trees, when one of the men shouted:

"Ular besar, Tuan! Big snake, Master!"

I walked over to investigate and found an immense python as thick as my thigh, coiled upon the ground. Its eyes were open (snakes cannot close their eyes) but it did not move at my approach. It evidently had just fed and was sound asleep.

It was so big I did not know what to do. I couldn't kill it with a stick. I had no gun. My surveying books said nothing about how to get around such an object. The Malays were too frightened to touch the snake and our work was at a standstill.

Finally I had a bright idea and asked my headman if he dared take hold of the snake's head. He looked at me as much as to say: "Why don't you do it yourself?" I then told him what I proposed to do and he decided to risk it. Very gingerly he lifted the head of the sleeping snake and laid it on the ground. He held it there very gently while I picked up my surveying pole, a red and white rod seven feet long and an inch and a half thick, made of strong ash and tipped with twelve inches of steel.

Taking careful aim, I thrust the spike into the

snake. It went right through his head and did not stop until it had gone a foot into the ground.

We all sprang back to see what would happen. Like a flash those huge coils opened up and started blindly lashing about. Now and then it would twist itself around a small tree the size of my arm, slowly bend it down and smash it. Despite the power exerted against it the surveying pole held. At last, realizing what was holding it, the python deliberately coiled around the pole and began to constrict. It cracked the rod into many small pieces which fell in the coils and remained imprisoned there. One of the breaks occurred just above the iron spike and the serpent pulled itself free. As it squeezed tighter and tighter on the fragments of the pole, it frothed at the mouth and oozed blood. In a few minutes it began to crawl away. Its progress was pitiful. Evidently the blow from the surveying pole had blinded the snake, for it collided with tree trunks and staggered. Each time it moved away a Malay seized its tail and dragged it back. In half an hour it was dead.

On another occasion I almost stepped on a python that lay asleep in a shallow pool. I fired several bullets into it with my revolver and as the snake uncoiled it grunted like a pig and glided away into the gloomy forest with its head at least two feet from the ground.

In "Pythons and Their Ways," F. W. FitzSimons tells a remarkable story of a python and a big barn rat upon which animals the snake ordinarily feeds.

"One day this rat was put into the python's cage where it heeded the python not at all. When alarmed by the approach of a dog or a person it hid within the coils of the python or behind its body, the coils being one on top of the other to form a cavity within. This was the rat's favorite hiding place and much amusement was given to onlookers by its habit of popping in and out. It lived in peace and harmony with the python for about three weeks, until one morning my Zulu boy requested me to come and see the python.

"During the night the rat had fed off the flesh of the snake where it was softest and most juicy, which was between the ridge of the backbone and the top of the ribs. For nine inches along the backbone the flesh had been eaten, leaving a long white seam half an inch in breadth. It was summer and the temperature was at least 80 degrees Fahrenheit, yet the snake, which was seventeen feet odd in length, allowed the rat to make a hearty meal!"

After one of my lectures in a Pittsburgh high school some years ago, the teacher in charge of the nature study class asked me to inspect their boa constrictor. Conjuring up visions of an enormous reptile, I entered the classroom and was shown a puny seven-inch snake. It was a boa constrictor all right, but a baby which had been found in a bunch of bananas. The class had been unable to find anything the snake would eat and even small pieces of steak would not tempt it. I suggested a live mouse, and after much trouble, one was captured and placed with the boa constrictor.

One day, having devoured all the available food in the snake's box, the mouse began to eat the boa constrictor, nibbling off a piece of the snake's tail. And to save the boa constrictor the mouse had to be released!

As a boy I remember going to the London Zoo to see an enormous reticulated python try to swallow its mate. Each snake was well over twenty feet in length. These two reptiles lived together peaceably for a long time. One day one of the snakes finished his meal of rabbit before the other and still being hungry, seized the hind legs of the rabbit protruding from the mouth of its mate. Before anything could be done to separate the two snakes, their noses met and one of the snakes proceeded to swallow the other one alive! After a few hours, there was only one snake of tremendous size in the cage. London newspapers printed daily bulletins as to his condition, and crowds of people visited the zoo to see the cannibal. But the unusual meal proved to be beyond the python's powers of digestion and after a few days it died.

I often have been asked whether I was ever bitten by a snake. The fact is, I always engaged a man to walk ahead of me in the jungle, so that if any one was to be bitten it would be he. One day, however, while wading across a river in the Malay jungle, I felt a sting on the ankle just above my shoe top. The pain was not severe until I got home. I removed my boots and saw two small punctures. Soon my foot began to swell, and in a few hours it was twice its normal size. I suffered agony. There was no doubt now that I had been bitten by a poisonous snake.

My mental condition was not improved as I remembered a friend of mine who had been bitten on the ankle. I found him in his tent groaning with pain and nursing what looked more like a toy balloon than a foot. He had neglected to take any precaution other than tie a string tightly around his leg above the knee. He very soon had an attack of fever and died in agony.

In my case, I immediately made several gashes with a razor blade across the bites and rubbed permanganate of potash crystals into the wound. Then I went to bed, attached a rope to my foot and suspended it until it was nearly at right angles to my body. In that way I kept the blood from running down into my foot. I remained in that position for more than a week while the wound constantly dripped. By that time I had a hole in my leg large enough to hold a hen's egg, and it was three weeks before I could walk. Months later the wound finally healed and I still carry the snake's two puncture marks on my ankle.

If I were asked, however, which is the more dangerous place, the Malay jungle or the snake house of a zoo, I would say the latter. Every day keepers and curators take fearful risks. I know one curator who actually allowed a poisonous snake to bite his hand so that he might test out an antitoxin. He very nearly died. Give me the jungle any day.

Don't confuse sea snakes and sea serpents. It is doubtful whether the latter exist, but I have been in swimming with the former. The waters of the east coast of the Malay Peninsula teem with snakes. They have flat tails, red and yellow bands on their bodies, and can hold their heads three or four inches in the air to have a look at you. Though they are poisonous, as are all sea snakes, they never attack unless deliberately interfered with. Sometimes you will see a large bird dive into the sea, catch a snake, carry him up in the air and tear him to pieces.

Sea snakes are helpless on land and tie themselves up into knots when they try to move. They are so common around the Malay Peninsula that when William Beebe wanted some specimens, he merely hired a boat in Penang, went out with a fishing net and dipped up a few. They grow to a length of about eight feet.

A famous American Admiral told me that when the American fleet sailed from the Philippine Islands toward Singapore, the lookout man was instructed to watch for sea snakes so that the fleet might know when they were in Malayan waters.

Of all animals, crocodiles are the ones I like least. No one seems to know how old they live to be nor their maximum length, though they have been caught 30 feet long and often have been seen 10 miles at sea.

The first thing that a native Malay does when he catches a crocodile is to cut open its stomach because it is often a treasure house. It is not at all unusual to find a complete set of jewelry—earrings, necklaces, brooches, bangles and anklets all ready for the next wearer. The man might even find a complete outfit for evening dress, including studs and cufflinks. In addition to jewelry there are usually a number of small stones. The older the crocodile the more stones are found. This is the crocodile's method of keeping his accounts. Every time he swallows a person, he swallows a stone—at least that is what the Malays told me.

Crocodiles are surprisingly agile and can run on land with amazing speed, lifting their bodies clear of the ground. They have been known, when annoyed at missing some indiscreet bather, to rush from the water and chase him.

The natives catch them in a very ingenious manner. A piece of hard wood, about a foot long, is sharpened at both ends. A long piece of rattan is then attached to the middle of the wood. One end of the wood is then bound very lightly against the rattan, and a large piece of meat, or sometimes a live dog, is tied to the piece of wood and thrown into the river. The crocodile seizes the bait, but the jerk on the line breaks the light binding and causes the wood to open out in the crocodile's throat and he is hauled ashore.

On land, the tail of a crocodile is its most dangerous weapon. He can easily knock a man down with it and usually knocks him in the direction of his mouth.

The teeth of a crocodile are constantly being renewed. His eyes, ears and nostrils are conveniently situated on top of his head, so that with his body submerged he can see, smell and hear. When he dives, he shuts his eyes and looks through a pair of eyelids especially designed for submarine work.

Sans Everything but Radio

CHAPTER SIXTEEN

OF all the East African natives, the Masai are the most aristocratic and the most feared. They had their origin in the region of the Nile River and before the white man came, were the dominant tribe. Today they number about 22,000. They live on a reservation under British rule, a closed district with armed guards at the borders. To enter the reserve you must first obtain permission from the authorities and must register upon going in and coming out.

The men of the Masai scorn work. They consider themselves the elite and, unlike many other men of the world, are successful in bringing their wives around to the same point of view. The women do all the labor. A wife is not only a servant but a pack animal as well. I saw one Masai man arrive at the local trading station with twelve wives, each carrying 60 pounds. He told me he preferred women to donkeys because women are stronger and can carry more.

Cleanliness is not an attribute of the Masai. About the only things they ever wash are their ornaments. While they take great delight in strutting about with the modest spear the British have substituted for the long, deadly weapon they once used, they are too lazy to carry their own matches. Nevertheless the men are never seen without a stout, short stick which is used on wives who try to emulate the leisurely habits of their husbands.

Masai society is divided into three ages. The first is the boy. The second and the highest of them all is the warrior. The third is the age of marriage which is considered "second childishness and mere oblivion, sans teeth, sans eyes, sans taste, sans everything."

The great ambition of every boy is to become a warrior. In the old days the neophyte had to prove that he had killed a man as part of the initiation, but the Government's ruling on the short spears changed that old custom. Every seven years, or thereabouts, the uncircumcised boys of the tribe are circumcised and taken in as warriors.

Having achieved this stage, the young Masai becomes a god. He moves into special quarters and lives with the unmarried girls. He usually chooses two or three little ones about seven or eight years old. He keeps them with him until they approach puberty when he sends them back to their parents to marry some ex-warrior. The only married warrior is the chief. Even he would not marry were it not for the pressure brought to bear by the braves. They, too, have discovered that a married man is more reliable than a bachelor. At the marriage of the chief, the warriors put on him women's earrings and a woman's dress which he wears for the rest of his life. His reward for wearing this humiliating attire is a grand funeral.

Except for the chief, little attention is given the dead. When an ordinary man or woman dies, he is carried out of the village and left for the hyenas to eat. They have similar tender feelings for the sick. If they believe one of their number is dying he, too, is thrown to the hyenas. If the sick man dies unexpectedly, they tie his body to an ox and drive the animal into the bush. The ox usually gets rid of the corpse and comes back.

Naturally, the Masai try not to get sick. Lockjaw is a disease they fear more than any other, and as a precaution against starvation in case they are stricken, they hammer out the two front teeth in their lower jaw.

Except for the warriors, the Masai remove all

hair from their bodies. Eyelashes and eyebrows are considered ugly and women pluck out each hair as it grows in. Babies are completely shaved at birth. The boys are kept hairless until they become warriors when they allow their hair to grow. At 30 they are unfit for fighting purposes and marry.

Don't feel offended if, when you are introduced to a Masai gentleman, he spits on his palms before shaking hands with you. It is his way of showing how glad he is to meet you. If sanitation means anything to you, don't invite a Masai to see your new baby. He'll spit on it, too.

Once a Masai has provided his wife with a baby she is compelled to wear many coils of metal wire from her knees to her ankles—her ball and chain. These coils are so heavy that they soon deform the legs, but she wears them to the grave. Many women voluntarily put the same ornaments on their arms as well.

While at an old East African Trading Post, I got an idea of the tastes of the natives by the amusing assortment of supplies on hand. The post was only a tumble-down shack and under its corrugated iron roof I saw in one corner large sacks of native bicarbonate of soda. In another were bales of native tobacco which looked like chunks of mud. The natives make a mixture of the soda and tobacco and chew it. There were also sacks of red earth, a crude dye with which the warriors color their hair.

Native honey, mixed with young grubs and wax, was kept in Standard Oil gasoline cans ready for purchasers to use for brewing good, strong beer at home. Beads of all sizes and colors, shipped from Venice, stood in barrels. The man in charge of the post told me that these ornaments were shipped in small quantities because fashions changed quickly. While I was there, the vogue was for red, white, blue and khaki colors but they're probably out of date by now. The Masai are style conscious and refuse to have beads or blankets of the same design and color used by other tribes. "Americani" calico was in great demand. The natives buy it white and dye it in a solution of red earth.

This tribe believes in a single god, named Mungu, who accompanies them on their nomadic wanderings with cattle that number thousands. While in the field they subsist on a mixture of warm blood and milk, the cattle supply both these items. To get the blood, the natives put a ligature around the animal's neck until the veins stand out, whereupon a tiny arrow from a special bow is fired into the vein. The blood then is collected in a bowl and mixed with the milk.

The wound in the animal's neck heals very quickly

and I never saw any of these cattle show signs of the many wounds inflicted on them. But I did notice that the animals were grotesquely and cruelly branded, their ears being cut into queer shapes. For about five head of these cattle, or thirty sheep or fifteen dollars in actual cash, a Masai can buy himself a wife. As he is a poor business man this is usually his best bargain. After that he lets his wife do all the trading.

It is hard to believe that there are shepherds in a country of leopards and lions, but I have come across Masais in charge of large herds of domestic cattle. These herdsmen present a picturesque sight with an animal skin over their left shoulder and their right free to carry several long spears or a long bow and poisoned arrows. At night they live in a ring of thorn bushes by which they protect themselves and their cattle from marauding beasts.

The poison on the arrows is harmless if swallowed, but it will kill an elephant if it penetrates the blood stream. To catch birds they throw arrows, the tips of which are fixed with heavy lumps of glue like wax. When they strike they stick to the feathers and force the bird down.

The natives do a good deal of hunting, for the simple reason that they like food and plenty of it. Their capacity is tremendous. Four negroes will

eat a whole zebra in the course of an afternoon—
and then fight each other for the entrails! We had
forty natives in our expedition and satisfying their
appetites was no small problem.

When the butcher in the marketplace kills an
old bull, shoppers collect in largest numbers about
the entrails. The latter are cut into pieces the size
of a walnut and carried home in earthenware bowls.
A good meat order includes a piece of heart, lungs,
liver, kidney, tripe and entrails. The greatest delicacy seems to be the stomach still crammed with
bright green grass from its last meal. It is sold by
the slice, grass and all.

Just as salt is a great luxury in the Masai diet, so
was it for our porters in the Ruwenzori Mountains
who would eat as much as three-quarters of a pound
of salt crystals a day. Others would make a ball of
dough with flour and hot water, fill it with salt
and put the entire concoction into their mouths,
swallowing it like a horse pill!

The natives smoke the strongest kind of tobacco.
In fact, they are not particular about what they
smoke. I have often seen a man tear off a piece of
his shirt and stuff it into his pipe. Once I passed
around some Old Golds to a group of them and they
broke out into terrible fits of coughing.

In Kenya and Uganda, native men wear a *kanzu*

which reaches from neck to ankles and looks like a Mother Hubbard. Unlike the clothes of many other Africans, they often are clean—except for the swarms of black flies that give the gowns a polka dot design.

Natives use their heads—but chiefly for carrying things. They balance anything from a banana to an axe with the greatest ease and I have seen them talk and argue without disturbing the load on their heads. In Uganda, as in other parts of Africa, the natives pay taxes. But any man with five children, all by the same wife, is exempt until his oldest child is ten. After that he must pay unless the same wife has another baby.

In Kampala, which is the chief town of Uganda, the natives are still under the rule of a *kabaka* or paramount chieftain. They still point out the place where the offending subjects of the previous *kabaka* were taken and left with their legs broken, to lie until the crocodiles came and ate them.

I once showed a photograph of the King and Queen of England to a chief who, when he learned that His Majesty had only one wife, asked in a surprised tone:

"What does he do with all his money?"

In the vicinity of the Mountains of the Moon, the Bakonjo hunters erect shrines in the forest to the spirits of the hunt. These look like bird-houses and are about a foot high and wide. The hunters take great pains to make the roof waterproof but the front is left wide open. When the shrine is completed a few pieces of peeled banana are placed inside and the skins of the fruit are impaled on sticks at the entrance.

Of all the interesting things I noticed among the natives, nothing fascinated me as much as their system of wireless telegraphy. While we marvel at the wonders of radio, these primitive people have been able for hundreds of years to spread news or send messages over hundreds of miles practically instantaneously. The art of this communication is slowly dying out and the younger generation of natives know little or nothing about it. The older men keep the secret of it to themselves and the actual code has never been revealed to a white man.

Their marvelous long-distance signaling methods have been more or less explained many times by travelers. Sometimes communication is affected by smoke fires, or again—as in the Cameroons—by the manipulation of a series of drums of all sizes so controlled that their sounds convey to the distant listener all the information that could have been brought to him in the sentences of an ordinary conversation.

But no one as yet has explained the real mystery

—the *veld* telegraph whereby neither smoke nor drums is used. During the Boer War, native house-boys told their masters in Bulawayo about incidents that had occurred around Ladysmith—some 500 miles away as the crow flies—on the morning after they happened. The greater part of the space between the two towns consisted of dense bush, great mountain ranges and utterly deserted open *veld*. No means could have brought the messages in time except the *veld* telegraph.

One of the most amazing examples of native news transmission came to light after a battle at Berbera in British Somali in 1903. Colonel Plunket of the First King's African Rifles had taken every available man from the depot at Zomba, over 50 miles from the southern end of Lake Nyassa, on a punitive expedition to Somaliland. The adjutant was left behind in charge of the post. At 3 o'clock one afternoon he heard a great noise in the married quarters and sent a military policeman to quell it. The policeman came back in twenty minutes to say that there had been a great disaster in Somaliland and that six of the company sergeant-majors had been killed.

Now Zomba is about 2,000 miles from Berbera and the battalion had been attacked by the Somalis at 2:30. Colonel Plunket and nine officers were killed and the battalion was almost wiped out. The news of the battle was received at Zomba within less than half an hour.

The following account of the same incident is also given by a District Commissioner of the village of some of the recruits as reported by Wilfred Bussy in the *London Daily Mail:*

These new soldiers, who were rushed, eagerly enough from their own territory into immediate battle, haled from the *kraal* of a paramount chief, which was situated not more than a stone's throw from the bungalow of the District Commissioner.

Two or three months after their departure the Commissioner was awakened one night by the sounds of a great disturbance in the *kraal.* The funeral drums had begun to beat incessantly, men were howling, women wailing, and even the children and the dogs joined to add their shrill notes to the prevailing din. The D. C., greatly puzzled—for it was evident that no usual tragedy of native life had taken place—hastily despatched a police boy to investigate.

"*Bwana,*" reported the messenger, "there has been a big battle in Somaliland and our company has been badly cut up. The fighting took place this afternoon. Sergeant Kanembe is killed, with a lance-corporal and fourteen privates. Corporal Ndoro, with two other of the N.C.O's, is badly wounded and hardly a man of the company has escaped without a scratch of some sort."

Now the news that was given the Commissioner that night could not possibly have reached him by any means known to Europeans for many weeks, necessitating the employment of telegraph, telephone, train, boat and runner. So he shrugged his shoulders, reflecting that many things are possible in Africa, and resolved to wait in patience for the arrival of the official news. In due course it came, *and the statement of the police boy was confirmed in every detail.*

The personal experience of Leslie Moore described by him in a recent issue of *East Africa,* a weekly newspaper, may throw some light on the *veld* telegraph. He wrote:

About two years ago I was working on a coffee estate on the Engare Olmutonyi, seven miles west of Arusha. One day my boss decided to take a few days off and go to the Mbugwe district after some elephant reported to be in the area. One morning, after he had been away for a few days, the estate head man, a native from Ufiume (about a day's march from Mbugwe), by name Kimwere bin Mgogo, told me that the *Bwana* Colonel had shot an elephant at 9 o'clock that morning. I looked at my watch; the time was 10:30 a.m. Naturally surprised that the news had come through so quickly, I asked Kimwere how he had got the news. With a queer smile on his face, he replied: "I have received news!" and not another word could I get out of him.

When my chief returned a few days later I learned that he had shot his elephant at 9 o'clock, and his story exactly bore out what Kimwere had told me.

This fact made me determined to find out how the news had got through. At that time we had a lot of Wa-Mbugwe labor, including some ex-K.A.R. *askari.* I was on friendly terms with these *askari,* with whom I used to talk. From them I gradually found out that Kimwere had the gift of foretelling future incidents in his dreams. All those *askari* told me at different times, and separately, the same story, that Kimwere had this gift, that he took no *dawa* (medicine), but just went to sleep after having his evening meal and during his sleep he can get the news. My present boy, Mumba, is one of those ex-*askari,* and he tells me that a lot of the Wa-Mbugwe are gifted in that way.

Kimwere's method seems to be similar to what we know today as spiritualism or "soul levitation." W. Marcus Falloon, in a long article on the subject in the same newspaper, is of the belief that this space annihilating power is a form of telepathy practiced through generations and carried to a fine art. He says:

The most expert in these practices have become most sensitive instruments and are able to radiate (or broadcast) what they wish. All the sensitive instruments (the initiated) are able to pick up these telepathic messages and give them out to their immediate neighbors.

We have come to look upon wireless as no longer a miracle. Why then should we balk at the possibility suggested above? I see no reason why a personality should not be able to transfer thought through waves infinitely finer than the ether waves used at present and that personalities equally trained and sensitive should not be able to pick them up. In fact, I am convinced that this constantly is done and that we are only waiting the discovery of the means whereby it may be crystallized and more universally used.

ADVENTURE!

Mr. Falloon went on to tell of a demonstration of thought transference he observed near Bukoba, on the west side of Lake Victoria Nyanza. While staying with a missionary the talk got around to the subject of mysterious powers of the natives. The missionary was convinced of their telepathic ability and offered to demonstrate it at the first opportunity. A few days later a traveler was passing through with his native boy (servant). The missionary explained what he intended to do and the traveler agreed to be a party to the test. The clergyman then took a piece of paper, wrote a message on it, sealed it and handed it to the traveler.

"This envelope," he said, "contains a message from my boy to yours. At 6 o'clock on the third day of your journey, ask your boy to give you the message from mine, write it down and open the envelope."

The traveler was able to cover a little more than 50 miles during that time. At 5 o'clock of the appointed day he told his servant he wanted a message from the missionary's boy. Between that time and 6 o'clock, when the boy told his master what the message was, the two men were alone and neither of them spoke a word. At 6 o'clock the traveler wrote what his boy had told him, opened the missionary's envelope and found both messages were identical word for word. The boys, who in this case acted as sending and receiving radio sets, were of entirely different tribes and languages.

The Leprechauns of Africa

CHAPTER SEVENTEEN

WHILE the Masai are the patricians of Africa, the pygmies are the most curious and the most interesting. They are probably the oldest race of man and have maintained their characteristics, habits and customs for thousands of years. These little people have played a distinct rôle in the life of man through the ages. At one time they probably inhabited Europe giving rise to widespread legends. They might have been the trolls of Scandinavia, the gnomes of Germany and the leprechauns of Ireland. The recent discovery in the north of Europe of the skeletons of a small race of human beings may lend support to this fanciful theory. Scientists may differ on whether or not these little people existed but there is enough Celt in me to believe in stories about elves and fairies.

On tombs at Sakkarah, in Egypt, dating from the Fifth Dynasty (about B.C. 3360) there are representations of pygmies which faithfully reproduce in detail the very features of the present-day pygmies of the Ituri and Semliki forests. The Pharaohs set great store by these little people, who played a prominent part in their court functions as mimics, dancers and entertainers. There is extant a letter from a Pharaoh, who lived about B.C. 3000, in which the most precise instructions are given to his agent, one Herkhuf, for the protection, comfort, and health of the precious dwarf he was bringing with him to Egypt. "My Majesty," wrote the Pharaoh, "desires to see this dwarf more than all the gifts of Sinai and Punt."

Although I have had little opportunity to observe the pygmies of Africa at first hand, I have some knowledge of a similar race of small people, the Negritoes, or Semang, who live in the depths of the Malay jungle. It was only by luck that I came upon them.

I had heard from Mat Noh, the Malay who was building my camps ahead of me, that he was employing nine of these Negritoes to supply logs for the houses. He saw them only occasionally and even then they usually ran away, although they knew they were working for him. One morning Mat Noh arrived where I had been surveying and told me that we were only a few miles from the base of Gunong

Tahan, the "Forbidden Mountain," the very heart of the district from which he had recruited his jungle men.

My predecessor had related that he had tried unsuccessfully for ten years to see the wild Semang, but his failure did not discourage me. I knew that if ever I was going to get a glimpse of the lowest form of human being in the world, now was the time to do it.

I learned from Mat Noh the location of the next camp site and armed with my camera I concealed myself among bushes and shrubs and watched the clearing—but not one dwarf appeared. I would return at frequent intervals only to find the place deserted. But, to my surprise, I noticed each time that the pile of logs had grown larger. I then realized that while I was watching for the Negritoes, they were watching me. It was a curious and eerie sensation, there in the quiet of the jungle, to be looking for creatures who seemed to have power to make themselves invisible. They were never far away from me. Sometimes I would discover where they had slept—just a lair on the ground made with twisted branches to form a rude protection. Once I came upon a large fireplace which was still warm.

I had about given up hope of ever seeing them when one day, while on my way back to camp, a mouse deer—a pygmy of the animal world—darted across my path. I knew I had no chance to photograph it but just for sport I tried to attract the deer's attention as I had seen the Malays do, by a leaf and two sticks. I made a blind, crawled in with my camera and began drumming on the leaf to imitate the mouse deer's challenge. Suddenly, without the slightest noise, a little black man appeared in the clearing. He was naked except for a small piece of bark and stood with his mouth open looking around in a puzzled manner.

I think he had heard my drumming and had been deceived by it, or else he thought another dwarf was doing it. Pausing for a moment, he made a peculiar noise and within ten seconds, in a most astonishing manner considering the thickness of the jungle, two women appeared each carrying a baby in a sling across her body. The man was not so heavily built as were the women, but none of them was more than four feet six inches in height. The women also were naked except for a diminutive apron of bark. They had thick lips, woolly hair, and were of a blackish gray color. Every now and then the women would jerk their babies up in their slings in order to get them in a more comfortable position, and the poor babies would pucker up their faces in agony and the tears would roll down. The most surprising thing of all was that the babies never uttered a sound and I could only conclude that they had been trained to cry silently. It was several seconds before I recovered myself sufficiently to take a photograph. The shutter gave a click. The man started and looked straight into the camera. Then one of the women looked behind her and, as silently as they had appeared, the whole family faded from my view, gliding with extraordinary speed and silence into the jungle. That night when the negative was developed I discovered to my joy that with the exception of the man's right hand I had succeeded in photographing the entire group.

Like the Negritoes of Malaya the African pygmies are woodsmen of the highest skill. They move through the tangled undergrowth of the forest without making the slightest sound. They climb great trees with the agility of monkeys that share the forest with them. Their huts of branches and plantain leaves are four feet high, with one small opening through which they crawl on all fours. These tiny houses blend so well with their surroundings that it is possible to pass within a few yards of a pygmy village and yet not see it.

The pygmies inhabit a wide belt of tropical Africa extending west of the great lakes for about three degrees on each side of the Equator. While true to type, "local races" can be distinguished by slight differences in color. The Akka of the Upper Nile and Niam Niam and the Wambuti of the Ituri forest are a deep chocolate red while the Batwas of Kivu and the Upper Congo are black. But everywhere they are quite distinct from the Bantu races who are their neighbors and who have driven them, in the course of the ages, into the forests where they now live. They are, indeed, as strange to the Bantu as to the white people who now take so great an interest in them.

The pygmies are purely nomad hunters, living on game, roots and fruits, supplemented by garden produce they obtain from their big neighbors. They are monogamous, in contrast to the Bantu; are never cannibals; have a horror of stealing; and, in the opinion of Sir Harry Johnston, show a greater intelligence than any other Negro race. Far from being "Nature's slum children," as some have averred, the pygmies are vivacious and adroit, quick to imitate and to learn languages, and cleanly in their habits. They have a natural sense of modesty and refinement, a real sense of humor and are marvelous mimics. Small they are, but not midgets. In height they vary from three to four and a half feet, and in weight from 53 to 77 pounds.

Of clothing they have no need in the sultry air

of the virgin, moist, tropical forest, but, curiously enough, they usually wear some kind of head covering—a cap, often quaintly shaped, of straw or leaf. Their weapons are the bow and poisoned arrow. The latter is made of reed "feathered" with leaves, and so adept are they as archers that they will loose three arrows so rapidly that all three are in the air at the same time and all will hit the mark. As hunters, even the lordly elephant is not safe from their attack. Aiming first at its eyes, they pour volleys of arrows at the great beast and follow it untiringly until it falls dead, just as prehistoric man did to the mammoth, and with equal courage and success.

There is little doubt that the pygmies originated in Asia, the birthplace of humanity, and migrated in the very earliest times to Africa. Undoubtedly, too, they retain some simian characteristics as they are clearly simian in appearance. They have broad, flat noses, short legs, inturned feet with the big toe widely separated from the four small digits and a covering of body hair. Emin Pasha records of the Wambuti that this fell is composed of stiffish greasy, short hairs and H. M. Stanley describes his dwarf of the Aruwini forest as having a fell of furry hair, half an inch thick.

They appear to have no language of their own,

says a writer in *East Africa Magazine.* Such speech as has been recorded is a modified form of the language of their Bantu neighbors but while hunting they have their own cries. T. A. Barns wrote that the speech of the pygmies of the Semliki resembles the calls of animals, especially monkeys, more than a language. They use intonations rather than words, particularly when calling loudly to each other in the forest. Their appetites are enormous, leading to that protuberance of the abdomen which adds to their ape-like appearance. One pygmy has been known to eat at a meal sixty full-grown bananas, with other things.

Their relations with the Bantus are, on the whole, good, a system of barter having been established between them. A pygmy who takes a fancy to a bunch of bananas growing in a Bantu *shamba,* marks it by shooting an arrow through the stem. When the fruit is ripe he gathers it during the night and leaves a present of game meat in exchange. Pugnacious and quick to revenge slight or injury, they are held in respect by the Bantus.

Homer, in the "Iliad," sings of a race of tiny folk in a far southern land, whither cranes fly in the Winter months. Herodotus, too, mentions the pygmies in his history. G. A. Schweinfurth, in 1870, was the first of the moderns to pay them a visit, and

Stanley, in his expedition for the relief of Emin Pasha (1887), gave fuller and more intimate details. Since then many travelers have had something to say about the little people, and for many years the Church Missionary Society has had a mission among them under the care of the devoted Canon Apolo Kivubulaya.

Martin Johnson succeeded in making excellent motion-picture films of the pygmies in their native forests, and he found them born artists.

Hell Below Zero

CHAPTER EIGHTEEN

THE story of the Mountains of the Moon, or the Ruwenzori Range, that snow-covered group of peaks on the Equator, goes back over 1,000 years. They were first put into geographies by Ptolemy, the Egyptian astronomer, and were well-known to Aristotle. For centuries they were comfortably ensconced somewhere in the middle of maps of Africa until that great explorer, Stanley, discovered them in 1889. Then a strange thing happened. The Mountains of the Moon were removed from the maps.

The action of the geographers in obliterating from the face of the earth a group of mountains which were well known to the ancients and substantiated by none other than Stanley, seems grossly impudent and presumptuous. But to get to the bottom of the controversy one must trace Stanley's exploits in Africa previous to 1889.

In his book, "Through the Dark Continent," in

which he described his attempts to find the source of the River Nile, he declared that he had sailed a boat right through the spot where the Mountains of the Moon were supposed to be. He further asserted that he was sure that the mountains did not exist. This threw the world of geographers into a panic. There was no one who could disprove Stanley for no one cared to penetrate the "hottest place on earth," which, at that time, expressed the popular conception of Africa. People wrote letters to the newspapers saying that Stanley was crazy and others wrote saying that those who maligned Stanley were crazy.

But in 1889, Stanley himself ran into the much discussed mountains and like a good sportsman, came back to civilization and ate his words. He wrote another book called "Darkest Africa" in which he told of seeing a great range of snow-capped mountains on the Equator. The whole world grew excited and travelers went to Africa to climb the mountains. When they got there they couldn't find the much discussed hills and came back to call Stanley a charlatan.

The sober element, however, went to Stanley and asked him if he had actually been to the mountains and he admitted that he had seen them from a great distance. That started the row and the mountains

CARVETH WELLS ON MOUNT BAKER, CENTRAL AFRICA, READY
FOR SUNSTROKE AT ONE END AND FROSTBITE AT THE OTHER!

were removed from the maps. A learned gentleman by the name of Cooley, wrote a letter to the great geographical societies saying that he would rather believe in the misrepresentation of Stanley than any such ridiculous act on the part of Nature as setting down a snow-capped mountain on the Equator—and in Africa of all places!

One reason for all the commotion is that, as a rule, you cannot see the mountains even when you are quite close to them. When the hot air from the plains below rushes up and meets the cold air from the icy summits, dense fog is formed which completely hides the range, making it invisible often for years at a time. Stanley saw the mountains by accident.

Another reason why few people know about these peaks is that they are uninhabited. You never meet any one from there and no missionary ever goes there because he wouldn't find a soul to convert. Still another reason that these mountains have been left in prehistoric loneliness is that they are so inhospitable. Situated on the border of the Belgian Congo and Uganda, they comprise a range about 60 miles long and 30 miles wide. Their western slopes are in the great Ituri forest of the Congo while on the east they drop down on the great rolling plains of Uganda bordering on the largest lake in the world, Victoria Nyanza.

Despite the fact that today we have fairly accurate knowledge of those much-maligned mountains, there are many persons who are still of the opinion of Cooley. They don't believe that there can be snow in Africa. I'd like to take those doubters with me to the Mountains of the Moon, stand them on the Equator and throw snowballs at them.

The mountains were actually climbed for the first time in 1906 when the famous Italian explorer, the Duke of Abruzzi, conquered them. He named the highest peak Mount Margerita, after the Queen of Italy and the second highest, Mount Alexandra, after the Queen of England.

When we climbed those mountains with the Massee Expedition in 1928, we found on the summit of Mount Baker, 16,000 feet high, a tin can that had been there 22 years. In the can was the Duke of Abruzzi's visiting card. Abruzzi's way of exploring—just leaving his card on isolated mountains—seemed so good that we left ours with his, along with a cake of Palmolive soap.

Osborn Goodrich, of the Milwaukee Museum, and I, started for the Mountains of the Moon from Nairobi on August 6, in a one-ton Chevrolet truck. After a day's journey we reached Lake Nakuru where without exaggeration we saw 10,000,000 flamingoes and ibises—estimated by the acre. They were standing at the water's edge so close to one another that the shore seemed to be a beautiful pink, coral and white strand. When they flew, they appeared to be a solid pink cloud and darkened the sun as they passed under it.

From the lake we traveled north until we reached the Equator. Then it was a steady climb along the world's dividing line for which the road is named, sweltering by day and freezing by night. I remember that I suggested that if we had cream we could collect enough ice to freeze it and have ice cream right on the Equator.

We could have slept at rest houses whose rate was $5 per day, American plan, but we preferred to pitch a tent by the roadside in which we slept in perfect safety. On the way to Jinja we had to stop many times to empty the radiator screen of butterflies which collected by the hundreds. Along the countryside in Uganda, we found red ant hills as much as eight feet high frequently in the middle of the road. Over some of these we saw a bamboo framework which we learned was a trap. Natives consider the ants, or termites, a great delicacy. When it rains at night they place a covering of broad leaves over the framework and the ants come out at the sound of the pattering drops. If they fail to respond, the ant hunter imitates the noise of raindrops by tapping on the hill with sticks. He collects the fat termites and takes them home where he eats them raw or fried.

Just before we reached Jinja, it began to rain and as we skidded gayly on the Equator, the rain turned to hail. The hailstones were about a quarter-inch in diameter and looked like tapioca. They bounced off the Equator just as they do in other latitudes.

At Jinja, we stayed at the Ibis Hotel, within five minutes' walk of the source of the Nile. The town boasts a fine golf course. The trouble with it, however, is that there are too many hippopotamuses on the course. One of the hippos attacked a friend of mine, on the Jinja golf course and killed his dog. He probably objected to the dog.

We crossed the Nile in a ferry crowded with natives and their bicycles. Each vehicle sported half a dozen bells, lamps reflectors and pumps. The African likes his bicycle to rattle when he rides it.

We now had 250 more miles to go. The roads were good and we speeded past plantations, golf courses and signs saying:

HOOT! GO SLOW!

probably put there by some Scotch engineer. Occasionally we saw a klipspringer, the chamois-like beast that can place all four feet on a dollar and balance himself. He is about 20 inches high at the shoulder with short straight horns, four or five inches long. On one road we saw hole after hole made by ant bears. They have bodies about six feet long, a proportionately long snout, tongue and ears, and short legs and tail. They live in burrows and eat ants.

At last we arrived at Fort Portal where we stopped at the Mountains of the Moon Hotel. It is 5,000 feet above sea level and is surrounded by a lovely, old-fashioned garden full of beautiful flowers where tame birds with gorgeous plumage flitted about: all in all an ideal place for a honeymoon. The owners probably had that in mind when they chose the telegraph address—Romance.

At Fort Portal we secured the services of George Oliver who not only had had considerable experience in the mountains we proposed to climb but spoke the language of the Bakonjo, the natives who live at the base of Ruwenzori.

He told me I must have 2,000 shillings in silver for paying wages. I got them from the district commissioner, Mr. Fisher. He gave them to me in an enormous sack that I could scarcely lift and explained that he had purposely placed the silver in a Government bag marked with a broad arrow, because the sight of the arrow would frighten thieves.

This money was to be left with the chief who lived at our first camp at the base of the mountains. He would disburse it to any one who presented him with a signed chit. This made it unnecessary to take money up the mountain and enabled us to pay off men whenever we liked, simply by handing them a slip of paper with the amount of wages marked on it.

By a stroke of good fortune I found in Fort Portal a copy of the Duke of Abruzzi's book "Ruwenzori," which I had been unable to procure in New York or London. With it we were able to follow his route and to plan each day's work as we ascended. Oliver preceded us to Ibanda in the foothills and when we arrived he had everything in readiness to start. He had hired native porters and had purchased food supplies and warm clothing for them. Our native food supply consisted of 70 pounds of salt, for which we paid $2.50; 1,200 pounds of millet flour for $17; a live ram for $10; a goat for $5, some chickens, and ten pounds of Epsom salts!

Antarctica on the Equator

CHAPTER NINETEEN

AT the start, the Bakonjo wore practically nothing except a piece of bark cloth around the loins, but each man carried his purse slung around his neck. This was simply the complete skin of some small animal about the size of a cat. The skin had been removed from the animal by pulling it over its head, so that it formed a bag. The two hind legs were joined together, making a loop which went over the porter's head and the bag hung down his back. A Bakonjo would be absolutely lost without his purse, in which he carries all his treasures, especially his pipe and tobacco. In addition to the purse, each man had a fire bundle and a peculiar musical instrument, which he could use either for entertaining himself or for signaling.

The fire bundle was most interesting. Three feet long and about 4 inches in diameter, it normally showed no signs of fire, but looked like an enormous cigar made of banana leaves. A loop was attached to the bundle, which was slung over the shoulder. Inside this bundle was a lot of tinder and dry grass, ignited before the bundle was tied up. In order to make a fire, one end of the bundle is opened, whereupon the contents immediately burst into flame. Fire can be carried in this way, in all weathers, for as long as a month.

The start from Ibanda was made in a terrific thunderstorm, about eleven o'clock on August 18. There was some delay until we agreed to employ the services of a Bakonjo witch-doctor, whose function was to control the weather and make the sun shine. This he accomplished by playing upon a flute. The doctor was a racketeer. Each native paid him part of his salary for playing on his magic flute.

Although food is unobtainable water is always plentiful. It is full of mica which gives the streams an appetizing sparkle. But when one drinks this delicious-looking water one gets the most uncomfortable pains in the stomach which can be avoided by taking frequent doses of Epsom salts. I carried 20 packages with me but it was not enough.

I have spoken lightly of the dangers of Africa's "jungle," but I must admit a great respect for the hazards of its mountains. When Martin Johnson and his wife climbed Mount Kenya they contracted double pneumonia and had to be carried down. In the Mountains of the Moon one has to keep warm and cool at the same time. And it is certainly no mean trick to guard against sunstroke and frostbite together! For three weeks we were either soaked to the skin with perspiration or deluged with rain. Wet at night when we went to bed, we frequently wakened next day even wetter. And during all this time the natives were paying the witch doctor to bring good weather through his flute!

In camp the goat and the sheep hugged the fire as closely as we did. They would thrust their heads as far as they could over the flames without burning their hoofs. The chickens perched themselves on the ends of the logs and sometimes had small flames all around them and beneath them.

The most exhausting and dangerous part of the journey up Ruwenzori was the crossing of the Fallen Forest, on the way to Bwamba Camp. For several miles we negotiated a huge tangle of fallen tree trunks, probably hundreds of years old, covered with bright green moss and very slippery. The slightest slip and we might have plunged down into darkness, to be impaled on a spike three feet long. Progress was slow and terribly fatiguing. Every now and then we would find ourselves on the very brink of a precipice hundreds of feet deep with a slippery path only a few inches wide along which our men scrambled with their heavy loads balanced on their heads. Then quite suddenly we emerged into the second level valley through which the Mokobu flows. On and on we plunged and splashed and slid and fell, until half a mile ahead of us, shooting horizontally out of the side of the mountain as if from some giant gargoyle, we saw a waterfall. This was Camp Bwamba, mentioned by the Duke. At Kichuchu the rain had dripped in a silvery curtain just beyond our tent, but in this case a great waterfall shot clear over it.

The color of the scenery around Bwamba Falls is weird. Large patches of golden and green moss mottled the precipitous sides of the valley. Sometimes, high up on the face of the bare, gray rock, could be seen an enormous slab of green moss as large as a tennis court. All the bowlders were completely covered with a vari-colored blanket of moss, while the water itself was a clear brown. Growing from a great carpet of gray, everlasting flowers, were vivid, green groundsel trees their trunks bundled about with great knobs of golden yellow moss.

The temperature that night dropped nearly to freezing, but I slept comfortably with a hot-water bottle at my feet. The next morning, in spite of the witch doctor's efforts, there was a heavy rain falling when we left Bwamba and started for Kaijongolo. At midday, with the sun directly overhead, we tramped through deep snow and were surrounded by "tropical" vegetation 50 feet high. Here, too, we found lobelias ten feet tall. As I recognized them, I remembered planting the same flower in the border of my garden where they never grew over a few inches high. To make things even more grotesque, the same groundsel I used to buy at a penny a bunch to feed my canaries, grew to a size here over 30 feet tall.

The next day, at exactly twelve o'clock, noon, with the sun shining directly down on my head—*I stood on the Equator in Africa with my feet in snow!*

Is it any wonder, under such conditions, that our porters clamored for warm clothes and called on the witch doctor to blow some warming blasts on his flute!

Before we went further we selected 20 men who were willing to accompany us above the snow line. Those who did not come with us were to retrace their steps down the mountain and return to the Bujuku valley with food and firewood where they were to meet us when we descended. The prospect of being immediately supplied with outfits of warm clothing caused the whole lot to volunteer for the snows. We picked out the men whose feet were in the best condition and handed each a fleece-lined vest, a woolen sweater, a pair of thick woolen stockings, a pair of trousers, and a pair of heavy boots or canvas shoes (whichever he preferred).

Trying on the boots was a ceremony that took three hours to complete. After much grunting, roars of laughter, and slitting open the sides of the shoes to make room for their little toes, they were ready to don their new garments.

Off came the filthy rags, animal skins, bark cloth, pieces of ancient blankets and dilapidated vests that some missionary had given them twenty years before. Each new garment was carefully inspected, then arms were thrust through trouser-legs and legs through sleeves, while the stockings remained an absolute mystery. When all of them were finally dressed they put on all their old rags over their new clothes.

The temperature was just below freezing, and as our goat and sheep showed signs of dying voluntarily, they were slaughtered. It froze hard that night and when the morning of August 23 dawned there was a dense fog. Everything and everybody was cold, damp and clammy, but I heard the song of a bird and found several spiders among my clothes, showing that there evidently was some life around us.

The porters had been sent on ahead, and by ten o'clock we caught up to them huddled round a dead groundsel tree which they had ignited. It was pouring volumes of smoke but no heat. Their loads had been dumped in the slush. Despite their misery and frozen feet they bucked up as soon as they saw us and were soon on their way. Not one of them had ever seen snow before and at first they carefully avoided touching it. The boots we had supplied them were strung around their necks and they wore their stockings on their arms. As the snow covered the ground they were forced to walk through it in their bare feet.

At midday, after a most exhausting climb, we reached Freshfield Col Camp at 13,930 feet, where we found six inches of freshly fallen snow upon the ground. Under the snow was deep moss and under the moss was several feet of sticky, black mud. Now and then one of the natives would sink up to his waist in the icy mire from which he would be extricated by the efforts of several of his companions. We were on the summit of a pass and surrounded by jagged, snowcapped peaks. The only shelter to be seen was a large bowlder with everlastings growing on the top and one large groundsel tree in front. After we had pitched the tent in deep, icy slush on the lee side of the bowlder we started both our stoves, filled our kettle with snow and served hot coffee all round, standing ankle-deep in freezing mud.

Later in the afternoon when we started for Mount Baker a dense fog descended upon us. As we made our way we left pieces of red cloth on prominent rocks and took frequent bearings with a prismatic compass, to insure our being able to find our way back even if the fog did not lift. The higher we climbed the worse became the weather, until finally at 14,150 feet we halted. All around us was snow about a foot deep and an icy wind blew the fog past us in long wraiths. We waited until about 4:30 hoping for a clear sight ahead. On the surface of the snow were crawling spiders and minute flies, upon which I presume the spiders fed, while fluttering about us were small brownish-gray moths, some of which I collected. They kept lighting on the snow where evidently they found something to eat. I have since heard from the British Museum that the moths are a new species.

The next day, after a night of misery, we made another attempt on Mount Baker. All three of us felt the effects of the altitude. Every few minutes we had to take a deep breath to relieve a feeling of suffocation. I had a splitting headache for several days and a severe pain in the neck. Late in the afternoon, while we were at the foot of a huge glacier, a heavy snowstorm started, with amazing suddenness, accompanied by vivid flashes of lightning and tremendous crashes of thunder.

Oliver led, I was roped in the middle and Goodrich brought up the rear. Cutting steps at an altitude of 15,000 feet was exhausting, but this was not our only trouble. None of us was provided with the proper kind of warm and waterproof gloves, and, as a result, our hands became not only numb with cold but also gave great pain as well. The snow was melting and soon our boots were filled with ice water. It was rapidly growing dark when we abandoned our second attempt to reach the summit and returned to our ice-cold tent, pitched in black slush.

Our food supply was rapidly diminishing, and it seemed essential to move the main camp and get the porters up from Kaijongolo and over the Freshfield Pass. But since Mount Baker was still beckoning, we decided to move camp and at the same time try once more. Word was therefore sent down to the porters and at nine o'clock on August 26 twenty-four men arrived. The others descended to Ibanda where they were to get fresh supplies and meet us in the Bujuku Valley.

ADVENTURE!

While Goodrich and Oliver set out for the peak
I started off with the rest of the men and equipment to cross the pass. By about eleven o'clock
Goodrich and Oliver reached the lower of the two
peaks of Mount Baker, locally known as Tourist's
Peak. Here a stone cairn was found inside of which
was a tin containing some frozen paper and a number of names. They reached Edward Peak at 2 p.m.
where they found the Duke of Abruzzi's visiting
card.

By seven o'clock that night we were all en-
camped beside a charming lake in the valley, leading directly to the Scott Elliot Pass. Around us was
a forest of groundsel and lobelia where many gor-
geously colored birds flitted about. They had the long,
curved beaks of the honey eaters, with brilliant green
and black plumage and a small patch on each wing
which looked like a glittering silver dollar. Both
sides of the valley showed rich, autumnal coloring,
while above the vegetation the precipices looked as
if they had been daubed with green and yellow
paint. On each side of the valley were glistening
glaciers from whose summits poured volumes of
heavy, white vapor.

On August 27 we began the final ascent to the
Scott Elliot Pass. As there was no trail for the porters, we led the way with Bamwanjala, our headman,

cutting down giant weeds, walking across the fallen stems of gigantic birdseed and scrambling over bowlders. Soon my heart was pounding like a sledge hammer, and I was not at all sorry when the porters announced that they could go no farther that day. Ahead of us was a great ridge of rocky peaks like a row of enormous teeth over which our route led. Our camp site was a ledge only four feet wide, but partially sheltered from avalanches by the precipice above. Our food supply was very low. Between us and comparative safety was that range of saw-toothed peaks. Beyond them lay the Bujuku Valley, where our relieving porters were to be with fresh supplies and firewood.

To make room to pitch a tent we chopped and dug and scraped, cut down groundsel, moved big bowlders and finally cleared a space about seven feet wide and fifteen long, into which we managed to squeeze our three beds. Then we put on all our clothes, crept into our damp sleeping-bags and tried to doze. In the middle of the night a heavy snowstorm came up, and every half hour or so a snowslide would slither off the precipice and rumble past our beds, missing them by inches and scattering snow in our faces. In the morning it was still snowing hard. Not a sound came from the direction of the porters, who were huddled together under heaps of rags and blankets. As soon as he noticed that we were up and about, Bamwanjala approached and started talking mournfully to Oliver. The men, he said, did not want to move. In vain did we explain that the storm might continue for days or weeks, and that the longer the porters waited the nearer starvation they would be. Nothing would make those men budge. The witch doctor blew his flute, and the snow came down harder than ever. When darkness came we were still huddled on the ledge, with less than a day's rations for the party and not a cigarette among us.

In the morning Oliver visited Bamwanjala, and from the grunts and squeals that came from the direction of the porters' camp, I concluded that he was warming them up artificially. The witch doctor, as soon as he realized that the *safari* was really going to continue, bargained with the porters for twenty per cent of their wages, in return for which he guaranteed to control the weather sufficiently to enable the expedition to cross the pass.

At 2 in the afternoon we started. My camera-man and I took our position at the tail of the caravan, together with the witch doctor, who played on his flute incessantly. At 4:30, at 14,500 feet, we were suddenly enveloped in a cloud. By the time the cloud had rolled by, five of the porters, including the man

SNOWBALLS IN HELL! HERE WE ARE ON THE EQUATOR IN CENTRAL
AFRICA. A NICE AUGUST MORNING, FREEZING HARD!

carrying my bedding, had lost their bearings and had climbed 500 feet to an unscalable cliff. Finally, at 5:30 we arrived at the summit of Scott Elliot Pass, and found the traces of the old Abruzzi Camp. Here we rested while I left some records in a cairn and collected a few specimens of worms that were living in the moss. A worm is about the only living creature I can think of that can enjoy life on the top of Scott Elliot Pass.

All we thought of now was to get down and back to Fort Portal, for our food was practically gone. More than 2,000 feet below was the camp in the Bujuku Valley, where we proposed to sleep and where our relieving porters had been instructed to wait for us. Night was falling and the descent had to be made in the dark. One of the men started to weep, and this started them all off. Blubbering like a lot of babies, they still struggled on with their heavy loads on their heads. I led the way, hoping to see a light that would guide us to the camp, and eventually found it.

After many hardships we arrived at Ibanda on September 1 where we were greeted by shouts of the native wives, whose husbands were returning to them wealthy beyond their wildest dreams. And when we pitched our tent once more at our starting-point, the chief was there himself to greet us, dressed in a white cotton nightshirt and a dinner jacket!

"Have you any message for the people of America and Britain?" I asked the Kimbugwe, whereupon he posed before the movie camera and made the following speech: "Tell the people of America and England that the elephants are eating up all our crops and our people are starving. The *safaris* come here and ask me to feed them. How can I feed them when the elephants eat everything? Come and kill the elephants, or we shall starve."

Where Angels Fear to Tread

CHAPTER TWENTY

THREE years after I had climbed the Mountains of the Moon, I received a clipping from the *Times of East Africa* in which my nineteen-year-old son, John, described his experiences while climbing Mount Kenya. I knew the boy was in Africa but I never dreamed he would attempt Mount Kenya. It is one of the most difficult mountains in the world to climb. It has been conquered twice and then only by expeditions on a big scale backed by large sums of money. John, although he did not get to the top, due to sickness which overcame him when well up, made his ascent on the allowance I gave him of ten dollars a week.

The boy had always wanted to accompany me on my expeditions and when I told him he first would have to prove his worth, he asked permission to walk around the world. In October, 1930, I left him in the remotest spot I could find in the British Isles —Lands End—with a knapsack, five dollars in cash, a passport and a promise from me that I would send him his allowance regularly.

Since then, John has made his way through France, Italy, Sicily, Malta, Egypt, the Sudan, Uganda, Kenya Colony and the Belgian Congo.

Because I continue to receive scores of letters from boys in various parts of America and England asking me how they can see Africa and the rest of the world, I am reproducing John's own story, purposely unedited, of his attempt on Mt. Kenya.

MY ASCENT OF MT. KENYA
By John Wells

After several days of preparation, I left Nairobi on June 3rd with the following equipment: One three-prong grapple, one ice axe (which I had to have made as the owner of the only ice axe in Nairobi would not lend it to me), one thermos flask, one pair gloves, one pair cross spikes for boots, fifty feet rope, Balaclava helmet and scarf, six blankets for boys and two for self, medicines and food for one week.

As I could not get a lift in a car, I went as far as Fort Hall by train, and a funny sort of train it was too. It took five hours to cover the sixty-mile journey, and moreover, instead of behaving like any ordinary, respectable train, it actually stopped between stations once for apparently no other reason than to allow a solitary Indian to alight and relieve himself by the trackside. On the way we passed many sisal plantations and saw them burning the old stumps. I am told, also, that the depression in sisal is so bad that many owners are burning the crops to make room for something more profitable.

I arrived at Fort Hall about 2:30, and found that the station was some three miles from the town. Fortunately there was an Indian there with a rickety old lorry, and he gave me a lift in free. Fort Hall is an ugly place, all corrugated iron and ugliness. I heard an interesting tale concerning the late founder of the fort. It appears that Hall was the officer who arrested John Boyes, the famous white "King of the Kikuyu," and sent him to Mombasa to be tried for his life. Not unnaturally, Boyes was extremely annoyed at this, and after telling Hall to do his damnedest, prophesied that he would live long enough to dance on Hall's grave. Boyes was shortly after acquitted, and a few months later received an urgent letter from Hall asking him to come to see him. But when he arrived, Hall was dead, and Boyes' prophesy was fulfilled. Not that Boyes did actually dance on the unfortunate man's grave.

I went up at once to see the D. C. but he was on *safari;* so accordingly I called on the A. D. C. and explained that I wanted to find out if I could get a lift of some sort to Embu, thirty odd miles on the route. He told me to inquire at the *dukas,* or Indian shops, which I did and promptly got a shock. At the first place I called the man wanted a shilling a mile for going the thirty-two miles and wanted to be paid the same rate for returning empty. That meant sixty-four shillings or more than half of my available funds, the rest having gone for food, equipment, etc. As I turned away sorrowfully, a trader next door who had overheard the conversation shouted that he would take me for seventy-five cents a mile, (100 cents=one East African shilling), but that was still too much. However, at long last, the same man who had brought me from the station agreed to take me for thirty-two bob all told. As this was the cheapest I could obtain anywhere, I had to resign myself to the inevitable, and told him that I would start next morning.

The A. D. C. had told me that in the event of my being unable to leave that day, that I might spend the night in an empty house next to his. So I went down to the station for my luggage in the local taxi, and thus made the acquaintance of what is probably the world's youngest taxi driver. He was a very small Indian boy, not more than ten or eleven years old at the most, yet withal an excellent if reckless driver. In fact, I was reminded somewhat forcibly, as the car rocked, and swayed round the curves of the narrow hillside road, of the biblical quotation concerning Jehu the son of Nimshi!

Calling at the A. D. C.'s on the way back, I was very kindly invited to have dinner with him that night, and breakfast the next day, to avoid breaking into my tinned supplies. In the morning after a fairly comfortable night in the empty house, I had my book stamped by the A. D. C. and set off in the lorry. (I should explain that I carry a little book with me that is stamped at each stage of my journey.) The lorry was a terrible, rattling old Chevrolet, that had done some thirty thousand miles before the speedometer had expired; none of the indicators on the dashboard worked at all, and she had no headlights, save for a hurricane lamp tied on with a string. Moreover, every half hour or so, the water in the radiator would start to boil and squirt out of the top, and we would have to stop and let her cool down.

We reached Embu at midday, and there I found that both the D. C. and A. D. C. were on *safari*, but I had lunch with the local agricultural officer, Mr. Hartley. Afterwards, I had the good fortune to get a lorry going to Meru, and calling on the way at Chogoria, the starting point for the mountain. He wanted only 20/- for the trip, so every one was happy. The road to Chegoria is very hilly and the scenery magnificent in many parts. Kenya itself was hidden in mists, and I got no view of it that day. We reached the mission about 6:30 and I presented my letters of introduction to Dr. Irvine, the missionary. Both he and Mrs. Irvine were charming to me, and despite the short notice, made a place for me at dinner and put me up for the night.

As I required only three boys to go with me, it was arranged much to my delight that I should be able to start about 10:00 the next day. In the morning I obtained the boys' food, which consisted of forty pounds of posho, some fat, and some salt, after which, the doctor gave me a lift up to Mborgori's camp, four miles away. Mborgori, by the way, is no longer chief there, having been sacked for looking on the beer when it was brown. After being photographed and saying good-bye, we started off in single file up the mountain. For the first half-hour, the broad track, which was originally made for motor cars, wound steadily upward along the top of a ridge. Then we went down hill and came to a river crossed by a fallen tree; I found it a most nervous business crossing, as my hobnailed boots refused to grip the slippery surface of the log. How the boys managed with their loads I don't know. A few yards further on there was a second crossing, but this time in a shallow place, where a boy carried me across.

Now we began to go up hill in earnest, and reaching the track again, passed on through thick woods. It was not unlike an English forest, and the resemblance was heightened by a kind of violet growing underfoot. An hour later we crossed another stream, this by means of stepping stones across the edge of a little fall about twenty feet high. Shortly after we halted for a rest and a little lunch, then continuing, plunged into the forest proper, climbing up a steep hillside, slipping, stumbling, grabbing at trees and halting every few moments for breath. About 2:00 o'clock, we reached the first big open space, covered with long grass and low bushes. Stopping here for a rest I was extremely annoyed to find that somehow or other, one of the boys had succeeded in losing the camera tripod, an almost indispensable article.

So I sent two boys back to look for it, and sat down with the remaining boy, who promptly curled up in a ball and went to sleep. About half an hour later, he woke up with a start, and looked about him in an uneasy manner. Then getting up, he walked along the path, looking closely into the bush. Next, I was startled to hear him give a sudden squawk, and dashing past me, he picked up a petrol tin, and began beating it lustily; then dropping it, he fled down the path with another squawk. I looked back whence he had come, and then began to move myself. About fifty yards away, coming towards me at a lumbering gallop, were two buffalo. I did not exactly run away but I passed that boy some ten seconds after. It was a most undignified retreat. About three-quarters of the way to the woods, the boy repassed me and then tripped over something, and I fell on top of him. Without wasting breath on bad language, we picked ourselves up and dashed on. Once in the woods, we fairly flew up the nearest tree, at a speed rivalling that of any tomcat! Here we crouched, gasping, and I fired the pistol which I had borrowed for signaling purposes (I do not ordinarily carry any arms). This apparently frightened the buffalo away, and we saw no more of them. Nevertheless the boy insisted that I stay up the tree with him for the next half hour, till we heard the shouts of the others returning.

When we had descended, I was further exasperated to learn that the tripod had not been found. I cannot swear in Swahili, so I had to content myself with making angry faces at them. The sun was setting fast and it was too late to push on, so the boys led the way to a camping place at one side of the clearing. It was on the edge of a hill, with a stream at the bottom, and so placed that it was highly unlikely that any buffalo would disturb us. Before we had supper, we erected a kind of tent for me out of a large piece of waterproof canvas loaned me by Mr. Hartley of Embu. This done the boys dined off a porridge of posho, fat and salt while I had beans and bacon. When it was quite dark, I saw that there was a great deal of luminous moss about, in fact it gave so much light that I put a heap of it in my tent for a night light.

Next day, after a night made somewhat uneasy by a large stone under my blankets, I was up with the sun, and found the boys preparing their breakfast of thin hot gruel. We broke camp and started about 8:00 and soon the tree where we had passed the previous afternoon was pointed out with grins and laughter! The laughter stopped, however, when a few minutes later we came on fresh elephant tracks, and a pile of still steaming dung. The boys were manifestly nervous, and were not reassured any when we came on fresh tracks of buffalo on the edge of an open space similar to the one where we had been attacked the day before. We crossed it with some trepidation, beating tin cans, and giving most unearthly shouts and howls. I feel certain that any buffalo who might have been near must have died of heart failure on hearing us.

Soon we reached the first of the bamboos, and at first it was not so bad. About midday, though, the path became completely obscured by a huge mass of fallen bamboos, and we had to cut our way with the *pangas*. So, alternately cutting our way, and returning for the loads, we progressed slowly along till about 4:00 by which time, the boys had apparently lost the way and we could go no further. We then attempted to retrace our footsteps, but again the boys lost the way, and by sundown we were in a position in which we could go neither forward nor to either side, and only a little way back. Obviously we would have to spend the night in the bamboo and, to make matters worse, we had no water whatsoever; once again I regretted being unable to say a few kind words to the boys in their own tongue. Then, the last straw, I discovered that they had lost the bottles of paraffin and meths, for the primus stove. At the sight of my purpling face, they scurried off at once and fortunately found the articles. On their return, they pitched camp in the tangled bamboos, and partly solved the water difficulty by tapping the trunks, which yielded a certain amount of evil tasting but fairly clear water. This I thoroughly boiled before daring to drink it, but the boys took no such precautions. However it seemed to do them no harm. Just as we were turning in, a parrot or something started to screech in a tree overhead, so I fired the pistol to make it go away. To my great disgust, it merely screamed the louder and in high dudgeon, I stuffed my ears with a handkerchief and turned to uneasy sleep.

After we had breakfast in the morning, I sent two of the boys out to find the path, while I and the other broke camp. About 9:00 they returned, having cut a path through the bamboo to the right track. We started and for an hour made our way scrambling, slipping and climbing over great walls of fallen bamboo. At one time the leading boy vanished before my eyes shooting straight down, just like the Demon King in a pantomine. He had fallen about ten feet in the tangled trunks, and we had some difficulty in hauling him out. The boys drew my attention to an enormous moss-covered leg bone, which they indicated by signs had belonged to an elephant. I wondered how the solitary bone got there.

At last we came out onto the old motor track; it was clear for only about 200 yards, both ends being obscured completely by fallen and growing bamboo. After a rest, the cutting was resumed, and in an hour's time we found ourselves on a fairly clear elephant track that led down into a valley and then up again, crossing another section of the motor track. One more phase of cutting, and we got on to a good path leading steadily upwards. It was apparently used regularly by both elephants and mountaineers for the surface was pitted with great, round sliding elephant tracks, and on each side were cut bamboo stumps. Now we began to see everlasting flowers and many others that I do not know the names of. Numbers of black, yellow, and white butterflies fluttered about, while the bamboos became smaller and more bushlike. From the branches of the trees hung long streamers of gray-green moss, giving an appearance as if hundreds of huge spiders had spun untidy webs among the trees and had had them washed down by the rain.

At last, about 2 :00 we came out into open country and I could have jumped for joy at leaving the heartbreaking bamboos. The boys grinned vastly, and I felt that the worst part of the ascent was over. Though this was a vain wish, I never wanted to see a bamboo again; as it is, the mere sight of a bamboo clothes pole makes me feel tired. The open space led upward to the crest of the hill we had been climbing and from the top we had a magnificent view across the plains. Ahead the summit was plainly visible, and no snow was to be seen on any of the peaks, it is very possible though that I was in such a position that the snow and glaciers that are perpetually there were out of sight. Below was the Nithi River, and we doubled down to drink of its clean, cool waters; they tasted like real nectar after the foul stuff from the bamboos.

After refreshing ourselves, we continued through scenery not unlike the Scottish moors, along a valley that led up to the peaks. About a mile from the Nithi we came to the first rest hut erected by Mr. Carr of Nairobi.

ADVENTURE!

It is quite a substantial structure, with four double banks
in the front part, and a kind of cubby hole at the back
for the boys. In the front part, I found two visiting
cards, one of a well-known traveler, Gaston Radio de
Radiis, and the other of Mr. T. Dando, of the *East
African Standard*. In a cupboard containing some tinned
supplies, I found the following amusing little poem:

> If of botulism apprehensive—
> O future mountaineers!
> This notice is intended
> To allay your fears.
> If sardines take your fancy
> Or prawns prove more your line,
> Rest assured they date as late as
> Feb'ry, twenty-nine.
> For they've been fully tested
> By one who ought to know,
> Who sampled them most freely
> For two whole months or so.
> But tho in sorrow I'd depart
> To browse in pastures new
> In every fish I'd leave a wish
> Of all good luck to you!

This was dated 21-2-29 and signed "Vivienne de Watteville," who, when her father Bernard de Watteville, was
mauled by a lion some four or five years ago, nursed him
for three days till he died; and then despite her loss
resolutely continued the expedition her father had been
engaged on.

There was another poem recording the visit of Messrs.
Soames Hook and Guest, dated March of this year. In

another cupboard were various tinned foods but I decided that discretion was the better part of valor, and did not touch them. I had no desire to become a possible martyr to food research!

I was feeling a bit tired out but attributed it merely to the height and the exertion of the day. After making a good dinner and taking my quinine I turned in early. A couple of hours later that same dinner walked out on me and I felt awful. However it still seemed to me to be a result of the conditions, and I managed to go to sleep. In the morning I was still feeling rather seedy, so I had just a little porridge, and more quinine, and we started about 8:30. Going down into the valley, we crossed a natural bridge over the Upper Nithi, followed the motor track, which here was in good condition and climbed steadily towards Hall Tarn.

About 10:00 the end came, my breakfast deserted me, along with a few odds and ends from last night's supper. I realized that this was something more than mountain sickness. I thought it was in fact the return of my late malaria. If I went further up, I would in all probability get worse so I regretfully had to abandon further attempt, and start back with all speed to Chogoria. About 11:00 we repassed Urumandi Hut, and after crossing the Nithi, I had the boys cache their loads as they seemed to think that they could not get to Chigoria by nightfall.

I knew though that it could and had to be done, so we went on with no loads to make sure. I was not in a state to take much notice on the way down. My legs were wobbly, my head ached abominably, and periodically I had retching fits. One thing I did notice though:

about halfway we crossed a column of bull-dog ants. Then I sat down and noticed things most actively for about ten minutes, till I had removed the last of the pests.

About three-quarters of the way down, the boys gave me the final shock. I had asked for some water, and they brought me my thermos flask. As I picked it up, there was an ominous rattling and when I opened it the inside fell into little bits. They had broken it. I was sick and tired, and I feel sure that I may be pardoned for the fact that I hurled the remnants at their heads and bawled them out in the best Billingsgate. Later I felt somewhat better, and continued in a rather mechanical way, till we reached Chogoria at sunset, and I was popped into a bath and bed.

However, this expedition has not by any means been an entire failure.

I went up the mountain not from any great love of mountaineering, but because I was after good material for my book, and I think it will be admitted that I certainly got it. For the first time in my life, I have been chased by creatures intent on killing me, and believe me, that has been worth the whole darn show.

In Columbus' Footsteps

20 BELOW ZERO CENTIGRADE. A REAL LOST WORLD, WHERE
VEGETATION IS PREHISTORIC.

CHAPTER TWENTY-ONE

A SHORT time after I returned from Africa, it was my good fortune to sail the Spanish Main with that adventurer of adventurers, Count Felix von Luckner—the "Sea Devil." In my opinion he is the most romantic figure to emerge from the World War.

His life from the time he ran away to sea at the age of fourteen has been a series of adventures. His father wanted him to become a lieutenant. When he failed to pass his examinations for that rank he was told, with some disgust, that he would become a hobo, and he decided to adopt the suggestion.

As a youth his ambition was to meet Buffalo Bill, and the only way to realize his hope was to go to America. He set out for the United States as a sailor on board a ship sailing by way of Australia. Remembering that his father wished him to become a lieutenant, young Von Luckner enlisted in the Salvation Army. But before he could reach any rank, he took a job as an assistant lighthouse keeper. Then Cupid intervened. The lighthouse keeper's daughter fell in love with the new assistant and as Felix could not reciprocate her gentle feelings, he threw up his job and set out once more to find Buffalo Bill.

Learning in San Francisco that his idol was in Denver, Felix walked the railroad ties only to find when he arrived that the famous cowboy was in Germany. Luckner swallowed his disappointment and kept right on walking from Denver to New York. He became a dishwasher in one of New York's leading hotels and eventually rose to be a door knob polisher.

Whether the next step after polishing door knobs was inspired by the Gilbert and Sullivan opera "Pinafore" is not known, but instead of becoming "the ruler of the Queen's navee," he went to Germany and passed his examinations as a master mariner.

While Germany was bottled up by the British, he volunteered to run the blockade in an old sailing vessel. Luckner, as history records, succeeded beyond his wildest dreams. After scuttling some fifty million dollars' worth of Allied shipping without taking a single life, he and his vessel were shipwrecked on the island of Mopelia.

ADVENTURE!

Taking an open boat, he sailed for forty days and surrendered in the South Seas to a British police constable who could not believe his ears when the famous "Sea Devil" revealed his identity. This policeman now is the Governor of Barbados in the West Indies.

One evening Von Luckner, Lowell Thomas, who is responsible for the "Sea Devil's" fame in America, and I were discussing the tactics of the old buccaneers. It was suggested that the West Indies would be an appropriate spot for the former German "buccaneer" to visit and so it was decided that we should all go. With us went General Dan Edwards, one of America's outstanding heroes of the World War. My good friend, Burt Massee, who had financed my African expedition, again came to the rescue.

Our vessel was the "Vaterland," an old American four-masted sailing ship with auxiliary engines. After running aground on a bar we managed to put into the harbor of Santo Domingo where we tied up at the foot of the main street. This sleepy little town has only one claim to fame and that is its jail where Columbus spent a good deal of his time.

Shortly after we arrived, the Archbishop of Santo Domingo, senior Roman Catholic priest in the Western World, came aboard in full regalia to pay his respects. He confided to us, among other things, that he had the body of the great explorer and discoverer of America in his cathedral. That was the first of many confidences given us about the remains of Columbus. It seems that he is buried in several places!

When news of our arrival reached the ears of the President, he invited us to have lunch at the palace. It was an elaborate affair. Count von Luckner and General Edwards wore all their decorations, and when they walked between a line of Santo Domingo army officers to the dais upon which was the President of the Republic, both were round-shouldered under the weight of their medals.

It was obvious at once that while the President was completely captivated by the "Sea Devil," General Edwards caused an enormous sensation among the Dominican army officers and he was swept into conversation with the General in command of the Republic's army. The last mentioned magnifico had his eye upon the presidency and in Edwards he saw "The Iron Man" who could run the army along modern lines. While the rest of us lunched with the Chief Executive, Dan reviewed the army which was waiting to overthrow our host. By evening Edwards had been given honorary rank of General in the army, title to twenty thousand acres of land and a house.

His suggestions about military affairs must have been good, because a few weeks later our host in Santo Domingo was deposed by Dan's General who now is President.

The night before we sailed from Santo Domingo, I engaged a native orchestra of five pieces to accompany us on our travels. I gave to each man an advance of fifty dollars to buy some clean clothes and to finance his family during his absence from home. At sailing time there was no orchestra. I mentioned the matter to General Edwards who sent word to the Dominican army chief that our musicians had decamped with two hundred and fifty dollars. Three hours later, as we glided past the old fortress which guards the entrance to the port, we saw a signal. It was to call our attention to five men, looking very sorry for themselves, lined up in convicts' clothes. They were our musicians—captured, tried and sentenced.

From there we sailed to San Salvador to see the actual spot upon which Christopher Columbus landed when he discovered America. We found it to be a British possession governed by the postmaster who is as black as ink. He invited us ashore to meet the only two white men, the Roman Catholic priest and the lighthouse keeper.

When we asked the priest to show us the exact

spot on which Columbus landed, he pointed to his little church. Only a wall tablet commemorated the landing.

"There it is," he said. "Unfortunately some Americans have erected a large monument on the opposite side of the island in quite the wrong place. I'd be much obliged if you'd take it from there and set it up again in front of my church."

It seemed a shame that so modest a memorial should mark the spot where the brave little Genoese mariner had first set foot on a brand new continent. We decided that by helping the priest we would not only do Columbus the honor he deserved but would serve society by righting an historical error.

The natives were vague about the nature of the monument. General opinion was that it consisted of a life size figure with a silver star on the breast. We were also told that on account of hurricanes the statue was wobbly on its pedestal and could be easily moved.

In the evening our ship's launch towed three boatloads of natives, who were armed with pickaxes, shovels and hammers, around the island. When our towing rope broke and left one of the boats in mid-ocean, minus oars, shouts of delight went up from the remaining two boats. As we were in a hurry to move the statue, we left the skiff behind with the men paddling with shovels for the rocky shore. About midnight we saw a flashing light and on landing were greeted by the priest in a very rickety old Ford truck.

Our party of thirty squeezed into the vehicle and drove several miles along the coast to the lighthouse, from where we started on foot along a sandy beach. A rocky cape, which jutted into the sea, was the site of the Columbus statue, and for at least a mile out were great reefs. It was evident that the only way Columbus could possibly have landed was by shipwreck. As if to bear out our observation, we saw a four-masted sailing vessel stranded on the reef, absolutely erect and fully rigged. It was sharply silhouetted against the moon about half a mile from shore. How long she had been there, no one knew. The priest and the natives were as astonished to see her as we.

Just as we started for the monument a wild horse suddenly rushed out of the bushes, galloped straight up to one of our sailors, kicked him in the stomach and disappeared. The recipient of the kick collapsed, fortunately only from a temporary loss of breath, and we left him in care of two natives while we continued toward our destination.

After a terrific scramble we reached the statue.

ADVENTURE!

Instead of finding Columbus wobbling on his pedestal, we saw a massive stone monument twenty feet high and weighing tons, with a white marble terrestrial globe set in front. Evidently this tribute to the discoverer of America was constructed to last forever.

It must have been the marble globe which gave rise to the story of the silver star which, according to rumor, so many people had tried unsuccessfully to remove. Running through the globe was an iron bar, about an inch thick and firmly embedded in concrete. Inscribed upon the monument was the following legend:

ON THIS SPOT
CHRISTOPHER COLUMBUS
FIRST SET FOOT UPON THE SOIL OF
THE NEW WORLD
ERECTED BY THE CHICAGO HERALD
JUNE, 1891

By this time we had lost all interest in removing Columbus and decided to let the Chicago Herald memorial rest in peace. We opened several bottles of beer we had brought along and toasted Columbus, the Chicago Herald and the priest who said that great newspaper was wrong. Thus having paid our respects to all concerned we returned to our ship. Our native pilot was so disappointed by the failure of the expedition that he drank a quart bottle of Angostura bitters and promptly became *non compos mentis.*

To add to the excitement already brought about among the natives by our failure to bring Columbus to their church, a seaplane arrived from America, alighted on an inland lake, remained a few hours and then returned to America. So fast a turn around excited even our interest and we learned from the priest that the aerial caller was the famous traveler and explorer, Richard Halliburton. Since Columbus was unable to appreciate what the years had brought in the way of speedy exploration, we gave the Catholic padre one hundred dollars to erect another monument.

Taking the hint from the mixup regarding the proper location of memorials, Count von Luckner decided to change the name of his vessel from "Vaterland" to "Mopelia" before leaving San Salvador. He tied a choice bottle of champagne to the bow in such a way that a man sitting on the bowsprit could swing the bottle down against the waterline on the boat's very fore tip.

A gay crowd was on hand. The appropriate words were said and the signal was given to release the christening bottle. Just as it swung down and skimmed the water the cheers on the tips of all tongues changed to "ohs," "ahs" and "I'll-be-bloweds." A barracuda lifted his head above the surface, swallowed the bottle and made off with a wicked wink in his eye!

Another bottle was procured, a watch was set for more champagne barracudas, and the "Vaterland" sailed out of San Salvador properly and lawfully rechristened.

Paradise Preferred

CHAPTER TWENTY-TWO

LONG before the cohorts of Ulysses tasted the lotus of the Nile or succumbed to the charms of Circe, men have dreamed and actually found their own paradise on earth. Small tropic isles, where Nature gives with a lush and bounteous hand, have crooked the finger of one hand and held forth tokens of ease, plenty and the charms of brown-skinned maidens in the other.

As the tempo of modern life increases to a faster beat, these isolated Edens become more and more a thing to be desired, so that today people wish for them and many sail away to find them. Yet few of these Utopias last. It is not within the power of white men to make an earthly paradise endure. For hand in hand with the dream goes the curse which destroys it. There is always a snake or a Lorelei lurking on the coral strands of a Utopian isle which eventually makes Erewhon no where.

ADVENTURE!

Gerbault, the French tennis star and lone circumnavigator of the globe, sailed his tiny vessel to the South Seas to found an ideal community. Rich captains of industry have sailed their great yachts to these enchanted isles eventually to return to the humdrum grind of their own world.

Commander Gene McDonald, in a letter to me from the Galapagos, told of the hardships encountered by a German doctor and his wife who left the comforts and luxuries of Berlin to emulate Adam and Eve in one of the islands off Ecuador.

"On Charles Island," wrote Commander McDonald, "is the most primitive post office in the world. It is just an old barrel stuck on a pole. Sailors from whaling boats leave letters in the barrel to be picked up by any one who happens to find them. Here we found an S O S letter written in German by Doctor Friedrich Ritter, explaining that he and his wife were the only inhabitants on the island. Deciding to have an adventure and lead the simple life they had arranged with a ship to land them and then to bring supplies to them occasionally. The ship landed them all right, but instead of returning later, it had left them marooned. They were compelled to fend for themselves in a Garden of Eden that was not so well stocked as the original. The letter requested any passing vessel that found the missive to fire a cannon.

"We fired our one pounder and used our search-light for a signal, but there was no sign of Doctor Ritter. Next morning, therefore, we organized two search parties and discovered the doctor and his wife. They were overjoyed at the sight of human beings. The doctor had a long beard and long flowing hair. His wife, also with long hair, appeared very young and attractive. Both were dressed in strange-looking home-made garments, but they confided to us that as a rule they wore no clothes at all, except shoes to protect their feet. When they heard our gun, however, they had put on the rags we saw them wearing."

Yet for all their hardships this modern Adam and Eve did not want to be taken back to their own country. They asked for food and other supplies which were given them, and they remained behind in the hope that some other ship would soon come along from which they could replenish their larder.

But of all the tales of paradise preferred none is as amazing as that of the British man-o'-war "Bounty."

When Captain Cook returned from the South Sea Islands with glowing accounts of manna in the form of breadfruit that he found there, the British government decided to introduce the fruit to the West Indies in the hope that it would increase the natives' natural food supply. To that end the "Bounty" was fitted out and placed in command of Lieutenant Bligh, who had been with Captain Cook.

The "Bounty" sailed from England on December 23, 1787, with orders to proceed to Tahiti, collect a cargo of breadfruit trees and transport them to the West Indies. There was no Suez Canal or Panama Canal in those days and a glance at the map will show what a tremendous journey the little sailing vessel had to make. On October 25, 1788, after a ten-months' voyage of 27,086 miles, she arrived at her destination.

Tahiti must have been a perfect paradise. According to old records, "In the course of two days, an intimacy between the natives and the ship's company was become so general that there was scarcely a man in the ship who had not already found his friend."

Instead of filling the hold of their ship with breadfruit trees the sailors languished in the arms of Tahiti maidens. So delightful were the surroundings that most of the men grumbled at the suggestion of work and expressed the wish to spend the rest of their lives in this wonderful tropical isle. After five months they finally bestirred themselves and sailed away with "seven hundred and seventy-four pots, thirty-nine tubs, and twenty-four boxes containing one thousand and fifteen breadfruit trees."

But even after they were well under way the men cursed themselves for leaving and day-dreamed of the sweethearts and other delights they were parting from. On April 28, 1789, the grumbling turned to sudden mutiny under the leadership of Fletcher Christian, master's mate.

The mutineers' plans evidently had been carefully laid. They had prepared a list of the men and officers they disliked and these were seized, including Lieutenant Bligh. They were placed in one of the ship's boats with a good supply of provisions and cast adrift. Altogether eighteen officers and men were in that small boat loaded almost to the foundering point. Twenty-five men including three midshipmen remained on the "Bounty" when it sailed away.

After many days of hardships and trials, Bligh succeeded in accomplishing a nautical miracle. After a voyage of more than four thousand miles, he brought his little company safely to land. When Bligh finally reached England, the Admiralty promoted him and sent him back immediately to Tahiti for another cargo of breadfruit trees. These he successfully transported to the West Indies, for which he was made an Admiral.

On his return to England, Bligh reported that the "Bounty" and her crew of mutineers had vanished. Determined to find her at all costs, the Admiralty outfitted the "Pandora" for the purpose. This frigate of twenty-four guns and one hundred and sixty men sailed for Tahiti with orders to search the South Sea Islands systematically, capture the mutineers and bring them back to England.

The "Pandora" arrived in Tahiti in March, 1791, and discovered that the crew of the "Bounty" had separated into two groups. One of the groups had taken the "Bounty" and sailed away while the other had remained at Tahiti and married among the islanders. Fourteen of the latter were captured, taken aboard the "Pandora" and placed in irons.

The captives told the officers of the frigate that after leaving Bligh and the others, those on the "Bounty" had tried to settle on a near-by island where they met with strong opposition from the natives. They finally had to abandon their struggle and return to Tahiti for provisions. On their arrival they told the Tahitians that they unexpectedly had met Captain Cook, a great favorite in the islands, and that Cook had ordered them to return for a load of food and live stock. The islanders, unsuspecting the ruse, not only restocked their ship but also donated eight men, nine women and seven boys. The "Bounty" then set sail for an island named Toobouai where the mutineers built a large fort.

Here again the natives objected strongly to this forcible colonization of their island. Considerable fighting took place. To add to their troubles, the mutineers started fighting among themselves and eventually the ringleader, Christian, decided to return to Tahiti and allow those who wished to go ashore. Those who preferred to remain on the "Bounty," would try their luck again at colonizing some other island. Sixteen left the ship. Fourteen of these were the men whom the "Pandora" found and captured, the other two having been murdered.

The mutineers on the "Bounty" thus were reduced to nine, and these, after dividing the ship's supplies with the others, recruited seven Tahiti men and twelve women, and sailed away once more.

The men who had been left behind on Tahiti did not consider themselves mutineers. They proceeded to construct a small schooner with which they intended to return to England. They even elected one of their number, named Morrison, to be their commanding officer and chaplain, and church services were held every Sunday with the British flag flying. Their little schooner actually was ready to sail when the "Pandora" arrived and took them all prisoner. Both vessels then set sail and began searching for the "Bounty," but they became separated and the "Pandora" herself was wrecked! Thirty-one of her crew and four of the manacled mutineers were drowned.

Boats were launched before the ship sank, and the survivors emulated the example of Captain Bligh by sailing thousands of miles to Java where, to their astonishment, they found the schooner which the mutineers had built awaiting them.

It was not until June 19, 1792, that the "Pandora's" survivors, together with their prisoners, reached England. At the subsequent court martial, six of the mutineers were condemned to death and four were acquitted.

Twenty years passed, and the mutiny of the "Bounty" had been almost forgotten when the British Admiralty received word from the captain of an American ship, "Topaz," of Boston, that he had discovered on a lonely island called Pitcairn an Englishman named Alexander Smith, sole survivor of the nine mutineers who had set sail on the "Bounty" after leaving their companions on Tahiti. Smith informed him that the ringleader, Christian, had purposely run the "Bounty" ashore on Pitcairn Island in 1790, where she rapidly broke up.

ADVENTURE!

After four years, the captain of the "Topaz" learned, there arose a tremendous jealousy between the native Tahitians and the Englishmen. The Tahitians suddenly revolted and killed all the Englishmen but Smith, whom they severely wounded.

Then events took an amazing turn. The widows of the murdered Englishmen turned upon their own Tahitian men and killed every one of them leaving Smith, the only man upon the island, with nine widows and several children to console him.

Smith at once proceeded to set his house in order. First he tilled the soil and planted yams, bananas, coconuts and plantains. As for hogs and chickens, they already were abundant. Very soon, Smith's family numbered thirty-five, all of them acknowledging him as their father and commander. At the time of the American Captain's visit, several of the men on the island were grown up. All could speak English, having been educated by Smith, who had turned out to be a man of great religious fervor. But England was too busy with war to pay much attention to the American's tale of Pitcairn.

In 1815, quite by accident, two British frigates visited Pitcairn Island. The captains, knowing nothing of the report made by the "Topaz" in 1808, were astonished to find, on what they thought an uninhabited island, forty people all of whom spoke excellent English. In his official report, one of the captains said:

"A venerable old Englishman is the only surviving member of the party that left Tahiti on the 'Bounty.' His exemplary conduct and fatherly care of his little colony cannot but command admiration. The pious manner in which all those on the island have been reared, the correct sense of religion which has been instilled into their young minds by this old man, has given him pre-eminence over the whole of them, and they look up to him as father of one and the whole family.

"A son of Christian (the ringleader of the mutiny), was the first born on the island. He now is about twenty-five years of age and named Thursday October Christian, because he was born on a Thursday in October."

When the warships arrived at Pitcairn, some people were seen carrying a canoe which they launched. As they approached the ship the astonishment of the sailors can be imagined when these "savages" hailed them in excellent English with "Won't you heave us a rope?"

The first man to come aboard was young Christian, six feet tall and naked except for a loin cloth. He was accompanied by a handsome youth of seventeen, George Young, who was a son of one of the

"Bounty's" midshipmen. Both men spoke pure English with the accent of gentlemen. When they took dinner with the captain, they placed their hands together in the attitude of prayer and said the good old grace, "For what we are about to receive, the Lord make us truly thankful."

On board the ship was a cow, and on seeing this strange animal, both men became alarmed and argued between themselves whether it was a giant horned hog or a goat, these being the only quadrupeds they had ever seen.

When Young saw a small dog, he was delighted and exclaimed: "Oh, what a pretty little thing it is. It must be a dog. I have heard of such an animal."

Being anxious to secure a first-hand account of the mutiny, the two captains went ashore to interview old man Smith, who met them on the beach and conducted them to his house. He was accompanied by his wife, now an old woman nearly blind. Both were much alarmed at the sight of the King's uniform. They were considerably relieved, however, when Captain Sir Thomas Staines informed them that the visit was quite accidental; that he did not even know that such a person as Alexander Smith ever existed, and that he had no intention of arresting him. Smith pretended that he had nothing to do with the mutiny; that he was sick in bed when it broke out, and that he had been forced to accompany the mutineers. He even offered to return to England, and when he made the suggestion, the members of his family burst into tears and begged him not to leave. When the captains refused to arrest Smith, the universal joy of these poor people was impossible to describe.

It is interesting to note that one of the mutineers, having worked in a Scotch distillery, set about experimenting on one of the local plants and eventually succeeded in producing an intoxicating liquor. Encouraged by his success, another man borrowed a kettle and converted it into a still. The result was that both men were constantly intoxicated and finally, in a fit of delirium tremens, one jumped over a cliff and was killed. This made such an impression on every one else on the island that all took a vow never to touch spirits again.

This amazing little colony has been left in peace. It has multiplied to such an extent that recently the Australian government had to remove a shipload of people from Pitcairn to another island to prevent overcrowding. Pitcairn Island has no criminals nor lunatics, and I often wonder how this can be explained by people who disapprove of cousins marrying.

West of Pitcairn Island

CHAPTER TWENTY-THREE

TOPSY-TURVY LAND really begins when you travel west of Pitcairn Island. If you reach the middle of the Pacific Ocean on a Saturday night, the next day is not Sunday but Monday. On the other hand if you go in an easterly direction and arrive at the same spot on Saturday night, the next day is Sunday and the day after that is Sunday, in other words a 48-hour Sunday.

It's a fortunate thing for the Pitcairn Islanders that their island is not situated on the international date line, because, being Seventh Day Adventists, they observe Saturday instead of Sunday as a day of rest.

Australia is the first of the anomaly islands that you strike. It is a continent bigger than the United States but with a population less than that of New York City. The country itself, as well as the animals, birds and plants is topsy-turvy. Rivers, for instance, instead of rising in the interior and running into the sea, rise on the sea coast and run inland to disappear altogether. Australian trees instead of shedding their leaves, shed their bark and the leaves remain on the tree. Australia is also the home of the duck-billed platypus, that extraordinary freak of nature which has a head like a duck, lays eggs and suckles its young.

Some Australian birds have no wings, others laugh uproariously, and another species attacks sheep and eats their kidneys. One of the most interesting Australian birds builds a large mound of rubbish and deposits its eggs in the mound. There they hatch without any further attention on the part of the female. A similar bird in the Malay Islands, instead of making a mound, digs a deep hole in which it lays an egg. It carefully stands the egg on end, covers it with sand and lets the sun hatch it. The egg is almost as big as the bird because Nature has constructed it to lay such a huge egg. When the egg hatches, out flies the chick into some neighboring tree having developed its wings inside the egg. This is the famous malleo bird, described by Alfred Russel Wallace.

Australia is the home of several kinds of kangaroos including some that live in trees, their babies when born being the size of a small walnut!

ADVENTURE!

It is said that Australia is the most ancient and primitive part of the world. Yet it is almost certain that birth control, comparatively new to our civilized existence, originated there and that the Australian aborigine was the founder of the science of eugenics. Australian natives have practiced selective breeding for ages.

North of Australia is the largest group of islands in the world, the Malay Archipelago, and here indeed is anomaly land.

Java, which looks tiny on the map, has a population of 38,000,000. If you go into its jungle you will find that the earthworms sing. Java is the home of the largest flower in the world, the Rafflesia— a parasite that has no stem or root. The Rafflesia is just a blossom that would make a gigantic corsage three feet wide. It weighs about fifteen pounds, smells of decaying meat and does so purposely!

Just off the coast of Java is the famous little volcanic islet of Krakatoa. Some years ago, Krakatoa exploded unexpectedly with such a noise that the report was heard in South America. Pieces of the island fell all over Europe, and other pieces went round the world three times causing the United States to experience bright blue sunsets! The sea around Java was so upset, that a wave started to travel around the world and was observed passing through the English Channel.

Across the Java Sea is the island of Borneo, covered with a dense jungle large enough to envelop the British Isles. Here live the Dyaks, probably the most notorious headhunters in the world, and orangutans, the most intelligent of the anthropoid apes. Blessed with very long fingers and immensely powerful hands, an orang-utan has been known to crush a man's head to a pulp in his hand.

Just west of Borneo is the enormous island of Sumatra, bisected by the Equator. It was here that Marco Polo reported seeing a unicorn, and described it as a "passing ugly animal." The old explorer undoubtedly was referring to the famous one-horned rhinoceros. It is said he heard that the horn of a rhinoceros was of great medicinal value and that he sent a small piece of it to the Pope, who swallowed it whole.

Sumatra is the home of the Menangkabou Malays, who practice the matriarchate. Here the head of a family is not the husband but the wife's eldest brother. All property descends from mother to daughter and not from father to son. This is a safeguard in case of divorce which is remarkably easy in Mohammedan countries. All you have to do in

THE FAMOUS NYINABITABA CAMP OF ABRUZZI IN THE MOUNTAINS OF THE MOON, WHERE WE SPENT ONE NIGHT.

order to divorce your wife is to say in the presence of witnesses:

"I divorce thee; I divorce thee; I divorce thee!" And your wife is divorced.

But if you divorce her lightly, you disinherit yourself!

A man can have four wives if he wishes, though a Malay usually is satisfied with one at a time. For real plural marriage, however, you must go to the Marquesas Islands. In that part of the world, polyandry is practiced, a woman having as many husbands as she likes. Here children belong to the community, every one is happy, and it is a wise child that knows its own father!

The Malay Peninsula, the most topsy-turvy place on earth, is just a short hop from Sumatra. In this wonderful island you will find animals that fly: flying foxes, flying phalangers that look like parachutes; flying frogs with feet many times larger than their bodies, enabling them to skim through the air on their soles; flying lemurs that look like cats, and flying squirrels.

The Malay Peninsula seems to hold the record for size extremes in Nature. There are insects thirteen inches long and others invisible to the naked eye; snakes thirty feet long like the reticulated python and tiny ones no bigger than earthworms; butterflies and moths a foot wide and others so small they require an expert to mount on a pin; large deer like the sambur with splendid antlers and the tiny chevrotain only about seven inches high at the shoulder; elephants and the smallest mammal in the world, a species of tiny bat. These are only a few of the amazing things to be found in the peninsula.

The backbone of Malaya is a great range of granite mountains. Mixed with the granite, in a manner that is a mystery to geologists, are gigantic masses of pure white marble, towering up hundreds of feet with vertical sides apparently unscalable. Yet on the top of these pillars of marble is a dense jungle where is found a rare species of small mountain goat. The marble masses are honeycombed with huge caverns on the roof of which are to be found millions of bird's nests which are exported to China and made into soup! Flying foxes by the thousand live in these caves, sleeping upside down on the ceiling, and forming deposits of guano on the floor, often thirty feet thick. Underneath the guano scientists have uncovered the stone implements of prehistoric man. Living in the eternal darkness of these caverns are white snakes, white scorpions, white centipedes and white cockroaches!

One of the Malay birds, the serindit, actually sleeps upside down. Another bird that reverses the natural order of things is the bustard quail. The female is larger than the male and very pretty while its mate is ugly and homely. She lays the eggs, of course, but he sits on them and hatches them. Strange as it may seem, the male of the bustard quail has sex appeal, for during the mating season, the females fight for the males!

The Malay Peninsula is one of the wettest places in the world. Two hundred and fifty inches a year is quite an ordinary rainfall, while nine inches of rain in three hours is merely a shower; nevertheless rarely if ever is there a real wet day! The rain comes down in torrents and dries up in an hour or so.

Monkeys and Malays object strongly to getting their heads wet in rain! My men were often caught in heavy thunder storms but while they did not seem to mind their bodies getting drenched, they invariably held a large leaf over their heads. They steadfastly maintained that rainwater on the head gave them malarial fever. I once drew their attention to some large monkeys that were also holding leaves over their heads during a shower, and they were horribly ashamed when I remarked that they used umbrellas like the monkeys.

The Malays have other topsy-turvy customs. For instance, when they beckon to a person to approach, they make the sign that we use when we want a person to go away and vice versa. I learned of this quaint custom the first time I camped in a Malay village and tried to change my clothes in private! As soon as I took off my trousers, a crowd of boys and girls collected. When I waved them away it was a signal for the whole village to assemble and watch me make my toilet!

Ants, too, have curious customs. Although the intelligence of ants has often been disputed, I have observed some remarkable instances of their wisdom, especially in the case of army ants. I have seen many of their armies on the march and in all the years I have lived in the jungle, I never could find the beginning or the end of the line. Where they came from or where they were going has always been a mystery to me. Rivers are no obstacles. On reaching the bank, the main body would wait patiently while scouts were sent up and down stream looking for a likely place to cross. I always noticed that these reconnoitering parties chose a bend where the current swept diagonally across the stream from one side to the other. As soon as such a place was found, the ants immediately formed into heaps several inches thick and slowly wriggled themselves into a ball about the size of a coconut. When the ball was large enough, it would roll in a most uncanny manner towards the edge of the river and deliberately fall into the water with a splash. As the current carried the living ball across, it kept rolling over and over, so that each ant received only a momentary ducking! Those that got such a ducking probably held their breath until they came on top. The instant the ball touched the bank on the other side it collapsed and the ants scrambled ashore, reformed their ranks and continued their march!

The largest true ant (not a termite) that I ever saw was about one inch and a quarter long and about half an inch high. These enormous insects always seemed to hunt alone. Their worst enemies are the smaller ants which often attack them and try to carry them away. I once watched one of these giants fight for its life. It was surrounded by about six very much smaller ants which maneuvered until they got a firm hold on the legs of the bigger ant. When one of the small ants would let go and take a better hold, the big ant would jump as if in pain. Eventually the little ones carried him away.

Those little ants were terrors. On another occasion I saw one of these tiny insects attack a caterpillar at least 100 times its size. When the ant bit, the caterpillar, like the giant ant, showed evidence of terror. After a short struggle and an attempt to run away the caterpillar suddenly turned on its back and died, having been stung by the ant. Leaving the dead body where it was, the ant hurried to fetch assistance, but before help arrived, along came a sexton beetle. This small beetle is another jungle mystery. You never seem to see one unless there is something to be buried. Just when the beetle had half buried the dead caterpillar, a small army of ants arrived. The beetle was driven away and slowly but surely, the carcass of the caterpillar was dragged away to the ants' larder!

While the ant is the fighter of the insect world, the seladang or wild bull, ranks with him in fierceness among the animals of Malaya. The seladang is not rare, yet it is one of the rarest prizes for the big game hunter and wild animal collector. It is said that a good specimen of a seladang would fetch $15,000, for a zoo.

The only trouble about hunting a seladang is that this sagacious animal objects strongly to being hunted. As soon as he has reason to suspect that some one is on his trail, he turns the tables on the hunter and proceeds to track him down. Many a man has disappeared completely after meeting a seladang. This great bull, which is probably the ancestor of all domestic cattle, will tear a hunter to pieces, trample him into the ground, roll upon him and mix him with mud until no traces are left! That's why so few big game hunters look for seladang trophies.

The Malay Peninsula is a paradise for followers of Izaak Walton, not only because there is excellent fishing to be had, but because there is enough material for volumes of the best fish stories in the world. Not only do certain Malay fish sun themselves in trees or convert themselves into balls for children to bounce, but others bury themselves in the ground where they are quite at home should the water in which they are accustomed to live, dry up. Fish, too, have been known to fall from the sky during heavy thunder storms.

Some Malay fish are fly fishers themselves! Many a time I have seen a fish wait patiently by the side of a large leaf until a fly settled upon it. The fish would then cautiously rise to the surface, shoot a jet of water at the fly with unerring aim, knock it into the water, swallow it and wait for another fly to come along.

One of the most interesting sights in the Malay jungle is the rain tree. In my six years' sojourn there I saw only two. Both trees were apparently devoid of leaves, yet water was dripping abundantly from every branch. Once I saw a distinct rainbow in the tree. The Malays told me that this water continues to drip for several days and when it ceases the leaves appear.

Talking about rain, Cherrapunji (48) is the wettest spot on earth. Whereas 900 inches a year is usual, they have recorded as much as a 1000 inches. There is some doubt as to the dryest place in the world, although Aden (14) must be pretty hard to beat. Many years sometimes pass without Aden receiving one drop of rain. This probably accounts for the enormous water tanks there which are supposed to have been built by Solomon in one of his wise moments.

The Sahara Desert, of course, is pretty dry, nevertheless, when the French government sank some artesian wells there, not only did plenty of water spout out, but plenty of fish as well, showing that it is not as absurd as it sounds to say that one could go fishing in the Sahara Desert. Fish live in queer places. They have been shot out of active volcanoes in South America, accompanied by water that was hot enough to cook them, had they been dead!

The old saying of "poor fish," does not apply to many varieties of tropical fish. In Siam (50), fish fighting is as popular as prize fighting in America. Many a Siamese fighting fish is as famous as Jack Dempsey. Enormous sums of money are bet on prize fights between professional fish.

ADVENTURE!

While we are in the neighborhood of Malaysia, just glance at Formosa (46). Most of the world's camphor comes from this jungle-covered island. It is found in the leaves and wood of the camphor tree and is obtained by distillation. While the Japanese are the camphor hunters of Formosa, the local inhabitants are head hunters, and many a camphor hunter has lost his head. The Japanese camps are often surrounded by live electric wires as a safeguard against head hunters.

IN CONCLUSION

AND so I have finished another adventure—writing this book. Twelve years of lecturing found me in another rut and I was anxious to get out of it, so my present adventure is radio. My next will probably be television, and when that is out of date I shall try my hand at something else.

All the explorers I know are restless souls; explorers are like sailors and the apostles—they have very little money but they see life. Personally I would rather see life than be a millionaire and if I had been born with a silver spoon in my mouth, I doubt very much whether I should have seen any more of the world than Florida, Southampton, and possibly the French Riviera.

Until I took up radio broadcasting professionally, I often wondered whether the years I had spent in wandering all over the world had been wasted; but now one of my greatest joys is opening my radio fan mail, because I then realize what a surprising amount of pleasure and happiness I apparently manage to dispense merely by recounting my adventures!

General knowledge and geography are the most neglected subjects in modern education. A map of the world is one of the most difficult things to find in many schools. If "Adventure!" does nothing but stimulate your curiosity or excite your incredulity sufficiently to make you turn to books of reference in order to check my statements, then I shall be satisfied.

AN APPENDIX

Of Strange and Divers Facts and Figures

Sea Serpents

THE possible existence of some huge sea snakes *is* believed in by many naturalists of repute. To dismiss the tales of reputable mariners concerning sea serpents as "yarns" is absurd. Less than thirty years ago, rumors of an animal with a body like a giraffe and markings like a zebra were not taken seriously. But since then the famous and rare okapi has not only been seen and photographed but actually captured.

Between the years 1520 and 1890 about 250 reports were made of sea serpents. In 1847 the captain of H.M.S. "Daedalus" reported seeing a huge sea animal over a hundred feet long and with a head like a lizard with huge jaws full of teeth.

A few years later a huge sea serpent was shot in

APPENDIX

Ballycotton Bay but immediately it was shot, it disgorged large numbers of fish, which when handled gave out terrific electric shocks.

If we are to believe in the veracity of Bishops, what about the enormous sea serpent observed by the Archbishop of Upsala, Claus Magnus, in the sixteenth century? This old church dignitary not only saw a sea serpent snatch up sheep from the tops of cliffs near the sea and then swallow a three-masted schooner, masts, crew and all, but he made a sketch of the incident.

Marmoset

One of my old schoolfellows at St. Pauls, Mr. E. G. Boulenger, collected a delightful lot of stories that would qualify him for membership in Lowell Thomas's "Tall Story Club." In the case of many mammals the father is anything but fond and is usually driven away from his offspring by the mother, for fear that he will eat his own children. But in the case of the marmoset, that charming little South American monkey, it is the father that takes care of the babies and not the mother.

King Penguin

Here is a bird that shares the family responsibilities with his wife. Mother Penguin keeps her eggs on her insteps and then bends down and keeps them warm with her stomach; she sits standing up, but when she gets fed up with her uncomfortable posture she makes a noise like a California jackass and immediately her fond husband answers the call, and, standing by her side, receives the eggs on his own insteps and continues to sit standing up until his wife feels disposed to relieve him.

Can Giraffes Make a Noise?

Most people maintain that the giraffe is absolutely dumb and cannot even sneeze. The late game warden of Kenya Colony, Captain Blayney Percival, has recorded otherwise.

European Toad

Here is a toad, known as the "midwife" toad, that carries around with him wherever he goes, his wife's small future family of about sixty eggs. He carries his burden twined around his hind legs for about a month, then he jumps into a pond and the babies emerge from the eggs and fend for themselves.

Darwin's Chilean Frog

Darwin discovered this topsy-turvy frog in Chile. As soon as his wife lays her fifteen or twenty eggs he promptly swallows them. The eggs hatch inside the

APPENDIX

father and emerge as nice little frogs (not tadpoles) that are able to hop gayly out of their father's mouth.

The Sea Horse

This strange little fellow imitates a kangaroo during the mating season and provides himself with a pouch in which his loving wife lays her eggs. He then swims around with his future family until they hatch out. The babies prefer the company of their father to that of their mother and immediately attach themselves to him by means of their curly tails.

The Bustard Quail

Here is a Malayan bird that is completely topsy-turvy. The female is larger than the male; she is pretty but he is rather ugly; she lays the eggs, of course, but he sits on them and hatches them, and during the mating season the females fight for the males.

The Chinese Paradise Fish

This remarkable little fish blows bubbles and makes them into a nice little love nest for his wife. He then courts and wins her, but instead of laying her eggs in the nest, she lazily drops them any old place and her husband has to follow her around picking up eggs and placing them safely in the nest where they hatch out.

APPENDIX

The Serindit

This is one of the most charming little birds in the Malay Peninsula. It is a small, green parrakeet, not much larger than a canary, and quite common. The serindit always sleeps upside down!

The Cacooy

Here is an interesting beetle, sometimes called the queen beetle. The insect is about an inch and a quarter long and carries a couple of lanterns just above her waist, which give enough light to read print by.

The Insect Duration

An enterprising scientist has stated that earth worms live three years, crickets ten, bees seven, scorpions from seven to twelve, toads even to thirty, but wasps and spiders are said to live only a year.

The Praying Mantis

Saint Francis Xavier, on seeing a mantis moving slowly along with its fore legs raised as if in devotion, desired it to sing the praises of God, which it immediately did in a very beautiful canticle. This is a famous legend about one of the most remarkable insects which lives on other insects. Some species are beautifully colored, resembling flowers. They will settle on a bush and wait until a victim approaches, then suddenly they pounce upon him and eat him.

APPENDIX

The praying mantis seems to have no fear of man, in fact in many countries it is regarded by man with the greatest reverence. In Africa should a praying mantis settle on a man he is immediately recognized as a saint. In Arabia the Mohammedans believe that the insect always turns its head toward Mecca. Some of the largest specimens of mantis have been captured in New York City but they have been introduced from Asia.

Bird's Nest Soup

One of the most famous Malayan birds is the swift (Collocalia) which breeds in countless numbers in many of the great limestone caverns of Malaysia. The same birds range from Northern Madagascar to the Marquesas Islands. Their nests are built from the birds' saliva and are collected by the natives and exported to China where they are made into soup.

Penguins

Penguins, although usually associated with the Antarctic regions, range as far north as the Galapagos Islands and have been found north of the Equator. One of their greatest breeding grounds is an island only about thirty-five miles south of Capetown, South Africa. Penguin eggs are served in South African hotels. At certain seasons of the year it is estimated that on this one island at least five million penguins make their nests annually. The local inhabitants of the district insist that when the time comes for the penguins to migrate to the Antarctic regions, each bird selects a stone and swallows it, in order to provide ballast on the long journey.

The Slow Loris

This Malayan animal often causes quite a lot of trouble between Malays and the police. Murderers often blame the animal for their crimes, asserting that it told them to commit them. The loris is blamed for all kinds of things, from broken romances to earthquakes. It has enormous eyes which it covers with its hands when exposed to light.

The Aye-Aye

Here is an animal rather similar to the Slow Loris which is also blamed for all manner of evil. It is a species of monkey with nocturnal habits and is found in the Island of Madagascar.

Mermaids

I have received many letters from radio fans asking me whether I was serious when I stated that there were mermaids in Aden. The legend of the mermaid is undoubtedly due to the habits of dugongs

APPENDIX

and manatees. Both these strange animals are somewhat human-like in appearance from the waist
upwards, and have a peculiar habit of raising themselves vertically out of the water, waist high. They
have breasts and hold their babies to them just as
women do.

The dugong is a marine animal and is found in
the Red Sea, Indian Ocean and Australia. The
manatee is not found in the open sea but in the
estuaries of American rivers. Scientists do not seem
to have decided whether these animals are land
animals that have taken to water or water animals
that are on the way to taking up their abode on land
eventually.

Fish Out of Water

I have been accused so often of telling "fish"
stories that I have collected a few fish that, with sufficient attention, might be kept in a cage. First and
most famous is the jumping fish which enjoys the
very highbrow name of Periophthalmus Schlosserrii;
this fish enjoys the fresh air and an occasional run on
the beach. It also can wink its eyes.

The climbing perch of Malaysia is another fish
that takes a breather in a tree and enjoys a casual
stroll across dry land.

Indian magicians often use a local fish known as
the snake-headed fish for their entertainments. They

keep the fish in a bowl of water but when required for an exhibition they take the fish out and make it walk about on land to a musical accompaniment. These same fish often live for long periods buried in the ground. Sometimes the pools in which they normally live dry up. The fish then frequently start out exploring the dry land for another pool.

The famous lung fish of tropical Africa and America can breathe air.

It has been found embedded in ground that required a chisel to break open, and have been known to stay out of water without inconvenience for three months.

The Angler Fish

This extraordinary fish is a follower of Izaak Walton and spends its life fishing for fish. Its fishing rod and bait are attached to its head. When fishing the fish opens its enormous mouth and dangles the bait invitingly in front of its own nose. Immediately a small fish takes a nibble the angler swallows its prey. In some angler fish the female weighs as much as twenty pounds but the male is so small as to be almost invisible.

Eggs

Here are a few interesting facts about eggs. A cod's roe weighing about eight pounds contains seven million eggs. The roe of a salmon contains about a thousand eggs for every pound the fish weighs. 280,000 eggs were found in the roe of a perch which weighed only eight ounces. Oysters are quite prolific. One oyster will produce from a quarter of a million to nearly one million babies; even this is regarded as a very small family for a single oyster, because one authority states that a single family of six million is not unusual.

Ordinary garden snails will lay as many as eighty eggs a day.

Two mammals lay eggs; the platypus and the echnida of Australia.

Animal Delicacies

Most people are accustomed to the idea of eating frogs and snails, but few people realize to what extent strange animals are eaten by the inhabitants of other countries. Monkeys are very good to eat and taste like rabbits. Flying foxes taste like partridge. American Indians eat the coyote and in South America many kinds of animals are used for food, such as the sloth, the agouti, the giant rat, the tapir, the armadillo and the great ant eater. In England gypsies relish the flesh of the ordinary hedgehog. Italians eat foxes, porcupines, robins and mice.

Sparrow pie is quite a delicacy in England,

APPENDIX

although it takes a lot of sparrows to make one pie. As a school boy I used to roast sparrows on an ordinary gas jet; they tasted fine. Germans eat bears; so do Canadians. Esquimaux relish rats and mice; so do the Chinese, who also eat dogs. Peacocks' tongues were regarded as a great delicacy in England in the time of Henry the Eighth. Iguanas are served in South America; they taste like chicken. Locusts, insects and many kinds of grubs have always been eaten by many races of people. The great traveler Humboldt reported that the South American Indians relish a meal of giant centipedes. While Americans eat enormous quantities of crabs they eat them dead, but the Chinese eat them alive.

Electric Caterpillars

The South American jungle produces a large, hairy caterpillar which gives a violent electric shock when touched.

Do Fish Swim?

Most people would say "yes"; but fish that swim with their fins are extremely rare. The sea horse is one of the exceptions and swims entirely with its fins. If you have ever watched a sea horse you know what a poor swimmer it is. Practically all fish propel themselves through the water by means of their tails and do not swim as we understand the word. The fins are used for balancing and steering.

The Only Poisonous Lizard

The Gila monster or heloderm is the only known poisonous lizard. It is found in Arizona and New Mexico. The patterns on its back are used by the Navajo Indians for designs in weaving their famous blankets.

Gila monsters grow to a length of two feet and are blessed with very short, stumpy tails. These tails are full of fat and serve as storehouses for food during famine. A Gila monster can have as many as fifty poison fangs. Fortunately these lizards are of a very lazy and sleepy disposition and rarely bite, although there are several cases on record of human beings being bitten with fatal results.

They Don't Do It

Snakes do not spring at you. Snakes can probably strike half their own lengths. That is to say, a rattler five feet long could strike you if you were within three feet of it. There is no such thing as a "hoop snake," which is said to place its tail in its mouth and roll along the ground at great speed like a hoop. Monkeys do not throw coconuts at people although they do pick coconuts, and have been known to throw them down; but no monkey ever took aim. Lizards in hot deserts, when running from one place to another, do not lie on their back and blow on the soles of their feet to cool them.

Animals that live on the sides of hills do not have specially short legs on the inner side, such as the famous "side hill gougers" of Canada. Elephants do not pull up large trees with their trunks.

Gorillas do not carry women into the jungle and raise families as suggested in the exciting motion picture film, "Ingagi," neither do hippopotamuses naturally rush through flaming forests and then leap from high precipices into rivers as depicted in another motion picture called "Four Feathers."

Lions and tigers do not rush about killing their prey in broad daylight as depicted in other famous films. Both are nocturnal animals and would have to be photographed by flashlight at night; but both lions and tigers will do almost anything you desire for the purposes of a thrilling motion picture film, if the animals are captured and starved and goaded to desperation.

Fish in Boiling Water

Several species of fish can live in water so hot that it would cook them if they were dead. Humboldt saw fish thrown up by a volcano in South America with water at a temperature of 210 degrees Fahrenheit.

Size of Snakes

No one seems to be quite certain about the maximum size of the great snakes, but I believe I am right in stating that the Anaconda is usually regarded as the largest snake in the world, growing to a length of possibly 32 feet.

The boa constrictor is said to attain a length of 31 feet and the reticulated python of 30 feet. Snake hunters and fishermen are very much alike when it comes to the measurement of their catches. I found the following information concerning the size of snakes in "Romance of Natural History" by P. H. Gosse:

"Attilius Regulus killed an enormous snake at Carthage and sent its skin to Rome. It measured 120 feet in length.

"Suetonius records a snake that was exhibited in Rome, measuring seventy-five feet. Diodorus captured a snake in Egypt measuring forty-five feet; Daniell states that a python sixty-two feet long was killed by his men in India; Ellis mentions seeing a Malayan python in Manila that was fifty feet long; Bontius speaks of pythons thirty-six feet long but the only absolutely reliable length of a large snake was in the case of Dr. Andrew Smith, who described an African python twenty-five feet long."

Ai

The ai or three-toed sloth of South America looks something like a very ugly monkey minus a tail. These animals spend their lives upside down, even sleeping that way. They travel about in the jungle, hanging to the branches of trees by their toenails and finger nails.

The sloth and the manatee are different from all other animals in respect to the number of bones in the neck. Whales, elephants, giraffes, apes, men and monkeys, in fact all animals, have the same number of bones in the neck, but the sloth and manatee are the exceptions that prove the rule.

Archer Fish

Another funny fish of Malaysia is the archer fish. He goes fishing for flies but prefers to shoot them. This fish waits patiently beside a large leaf growing close to the water, until some unwary fly settles upon it.

The fish then rises to the surface, takes careful aim and shoots the fly with a jet of water, knocking it into the water. It then swallows the fly and waits for another to come along.

APPENDIX

Adjutant Bird

This amusing bird is the largest of the storks. He has a rapacious appetite and powerful digestion. Not only does the bird eat tortoises and snakes but has been known to swallow a live cat. In India the bird is protected because it is so useful in disposing of garbage.

CARVETH WELLS' MAP OF

1. **ENGLAND.**
2. **IRELAND.** *The Blarney Stone here.*
3. **LAPLAND.** *The summer home of Santa Claus. Lemmings commit suicide here!*
4. **SCANDINAVIA.** *Home of the Swedish Bath.*
5. **GIBRALTAR.** *Barbary Apes here. Oranges and Spaniards.*
6. **ALGIERS,** *where France is trying to civilize the A-rabs.*
7. **DAMASCUS.** *One of the holy cities of Islam. Home of Ananias!*
8. **PARIS.** *Enough said.*
9. **MALTA.** *Cats.*
10. **BAGDAD.** *Arabian Nights.*

11. **JERUSALEM.** *Where Abraham was going to offer up Isaac.*
12. **CAIRO.** *Made famous by Shepheards Hotel.*
13. **MECCA.** *Closed to Christians.*
14. **ADEN.** *Mermaids here!*
15. **CEYLON.** *Made famous by Lipton.*
16. **MOUNT EVEREST.** *Highest mountain in the world.*
17. **KERGUELEN ISLAND.** *Captain Cook found cabbages growing here.*
18. **CAPE** *inha light*
19. **MOM** *game*

20. **NAIROBI.** *Where the big game hunters outfit.*
21. **JINJA.** *Good golf course here; hippos on the greens.*
22. **MOUNTAINS OF THE MOON.**
23. **CAPE TOWN.** *Oranges her.*
24. **MADEIRA.** *Christopher Columbus was married here.*
25. **THE AMAZON JUNGLE.**
26. **BERMUDA.** *Where rainbows begin.*
27. **SANTO DOMINGO.** *Where Christopher Columbus was put in jail. His body supposed to be here in the Cathedral.*
28. **SAN SALVADOR.** *Both Christopher Columbus and Richard Halliburton landed here.*
29. **JAMAICA.** *Rum and ginger*

F THE WORLD

30. **GALAPAGOS ISLANDS.** *Penguins, giant tortoises and sea lizards.*

31. **MONTREAL.** *Where I first landed on the American Continent.*

32. **NEW YORK.** *No place on earth like it.*

33. **JAMESTOWN, VA.** *First British Colonists. Princess Pocahontas.*

34. **CHICAGO.** *Where Al Capone hangs out.*

35. **WINNIPEG.**

36. **PEACE RIVER CROSSING.** *Canada's Last Great West.*

37. **PRINCE RUPERT.** *Terminus of Grand Trunk Pacific Railway.*

38. **PORTLAND.** *Apples here.*

39. **SAN FRANCISCO.** *The Golden Gate.*

40. **NASSAU.** *An American Oasis.*

41. **GOBI DESERT.** *Dinosaur Eggs here.*

42. **VERKHOIANSK.** *Coldest spot on earth.*

43. **WRANGELL ISLAND.** *Rather inhospitable place.*

44. **PRIBILOF ISLANDS.** *Breeding place of Fur Seals.*

45. **TOKIO.**

46. **FORMOSA.** *Head Hunters and camphor.*

47. **HONG KONG.**

48. **CHERRAPUNJI.** *The wettest spot on earth. 1000 inches a year.*

49. **MERGUI ARCHIPELAGO.** *Sea Gypsies live here.*

50. **BANGKOK.** *Home of the White Elephant.*

51. **SINGAPORE.** *Paradise for beach combers!*

52. **BORNEO.** *Orang Utans here.*

53. **JAVA.** *Earth worms sing here.*

54. **COCOS ISLANDS.** *Crabs eat coconuts here.*

55. **AUSTRALIA.** *Home of the Duckbilled Platypus.*

57. **HAWAII.** *Hula hula girls here.*

58. **MARQUESAS ISLANDS.** *Girls have as many husbands as they like here.*

59. **PITCAIRN ISLAND.** *All Seventh Day Adventists here.*

www.ingramcontent.com/pod-product-compliance
Lightning Source LLC
Chambersburg PA
CBHW071355150726
48000CB00001B/35